Twenty Reasons Not To Garden

(And Why I Ignore Them All)

By: Luke Ruggenberg

For my girls.

Table of Contents

Foreword..7
Reason #1: The Toy Box...9
Reason #2: Like the Cleaning of a House ... .15
Reason #3: The Case of Michael R. Clancy-Dubuquesne
McGumbyton III..22
Reason #4: Pop the Trunk...31
Reason #5: Gold-Digger..40
Reason #6: Name ... That ... Plant!...............................47
Reason #7: The Asylum...56
Reason #8: Two Days, Max..63
Reason #9: The Service Was Terrible............................69
Reason #10: The Red-Handled Devils...........................75
Reason #11: Zero Chance of Iced Teastorms................80
Reason #12: The Green Reaper......................................86
Reason #13: Bread Season..93
Reason #14: Triage..101
Reason #15: WHAT IS 7?...109
Reason #16: Self-Defense..117
Reason #17: You're Doing it Wrong............................126
Reason #18: Paparazzi...135
Reason #19: Harbingers...142
Reason #20: I Can Quit Any Time...............................146

Foreword

Gardening is just the worst. What? Why does no one believe me when I say that?

"If gardening is so bad," they protest, "why have you been hacking away at it your entire adult life?"

The answer is simple: no one bothered telling *me* that gardening is the worst. I had no idea what I was getting into. Now, after so long in the field, I'm not even sure if I like it anymore. All I know is that I can't stop gardening any more than I could stop wearing pants. And I know what you're thinking, but you don't want to see this guy in a kilt.

No, sadly it's too late for yours truly, but for any of you who may be on the gardening fence (which may or may not be an actual fence, by the way—you'll quickly learn to distrust metaphor in this business), there may yet be time to save yourself. Go on. Get out now. Trust me, you don't want any part of this. There are slugs and sunburns and various *mildews* and—ugh—well, we'll get into all that. For now, heed well this advice: quit tinkering with raised beds or trying on wide-brimmed hats and just take up knitting. You'll thank me in the long run. You don't even have to read this book if you simply go out right now and trade in that shiny new trowel for a skein of yarn. Yeah, I'm pretty sure you can do that down at Fred Meyer.

...

As for all you who have stuck around, you're just like every other gardener I've ever known: stubborn as a stump. Very well then, read on, and may you get what you deserve. Don't say I didn't warn you.

-L.R.

Reason #1:

The Toy Box

Trying to picture yourself as a gardener? Maybe you've only gotten as far as the hat before stalling. It is quite a hat. Don't worry, they all look silly. The hat is practical, the rest of gardening, by and large, is not.

If you are like most gardeners, you will at some point, if only briefly, entertain the thought of yourself as a great artist: the earth and its plants your media, the landscape your canvas, the garden your legacy to mankind. You will do research. You will measure and sketch and plan. You will strive to create a dialogue between your garden and its natural or urban surroundings. You will squint and stand back and employ gravitas in your plant selections, with one eye always on the big picture: the composition of your *masterpiece*. You will be driven by subtlety. You will be moved by grace. Above all, you will show restraint.

And once you fail at each of these things, you can set about being a real gardener. Because somewhere along the way, you will surely lose the forest for the trees. More accurately, you will lose the forest for the trees and the shrubs and the vines and perennials and annuals and new cultivars and hybrids and—A *PINK* BLUEBERRY? OMG! MUST HAVE—and, well, you get the idea. As the allure of individual plants becomes stronger, it will begin to cloud your grand vision with base and immediate desire. And even though you may be drawn to these certain plants by their aesthetic appeal, the course of your plant acquisition will no more be mistaken for artistry than would a raven collecting shiny objects. Make no mistake, as your self-restraint crumbles, your painter's pallet, once dabbed and smeared with promising hues and textures, will become just another surface on which to set the plants you can't seem to stop hoarding and for which you have long since run out of room.

Which is not to say that gardening cannot be an artistic endeavor. There are plenty of gardeners who are able to envision and realize beautiful landscapes, which are composed over the span of years with prudence and toil and boundless inspiration. All gardeners, in their desire to create something nice to look at, do occasionally don the artist's frock (more likely some sort of vest, in our case). But it is far more often true, especially when confronted with acres of titillating plants for sale, that the measured, squinting plant *artiste* is unceremoniously shoved aside and trampled by the plant *collector,* like a big kid bowling over toddlers in a toy store. This is the image you should perhaps conjure when picturing yourself as a gardener—but still with a hat.

For collecting plants is not inherently different from collecting toys, or shoes, or shells, or nineteenth century German glockenspiels. Like so many of our compulsions, it is a teasing, seldom-fulfilling endeavor spurred on by the poorly translated urges of an over-evolved ape.

To really get in the head-space of a gardener, try to think back to when you were a kid watching Saturday morning cartoons—watching Saturday morning commercials, that is. Toys and toys and toys and tough-guy narrations for action figures over skull-crushing jingles; princesses and ponies and everything the same cloying pink; RC cars; elaborate injection-molded play-sets; songs promising school-cred coolness if you go ask your parents *right now!* for a back-mounted water cannon system with more PSI than anything employed by the local fire department.

You want it all. Everything. How can you not? It's all awesome. Look at the kids on the ads: they're so happy, so existentially complete with their new talking, articulated, glow-in-the-dark spider monster ... thing. This one SHOOTS A WEB, for crying out loud. You need it because you have been made aware of it. Its absence is felt as though it were something once yours but tragically lost. You must have it *back* if you are ever to feel whole again. Maybe you already have several other talking arachnids in your toy box—who cares, those mean *nothing* because this new one SHOOTS A WEB!

And that's just the glowing spider. The toy ads are a relentless siege, which pauses only to reload during brief spells of token programming. You are pummeled with desire.

Now, let's take this a bit further and say that not only do you want it all, but due to some anomalously indulgent parents, you are allowed to *have* it all. Any toy you want is yours, so long as it fits in your toy box. That's right, once a week, your suspiciously generous folks (targets of rabid jealousy the school over), drive you to the toy store and just turn you loose. It doesn't even matter that your toy box is overflowing. When you get home, you'll just throw away some old toys to make room for the new.

As you run giggling up and down the aisles—snatching toys off the shelves, hyperventilating, straining your little muscles reaching for everything at once—perhaps the occasional thought pops into your head that one of these new toys might be a fun addition to some cadre of similarly themed toys you have at home. Maybe you can put the finishing touches on that army of glow-in-the-dark beasties or shore-up your aquatic payload capability. But mostly, rather than putting together a pleasing and synergistic assortment of toys, you're just lunging for any awesome thing you saw on TV. You are capricious and spoilt. You are greed run amok. You are a little hellion who gets what he/she wants and wants what she/he sees.

This is the picture of the gardener you will, in all likelihood, become. Less artist and more spoiled kid stuffing your garden toy box with every pretty leaf or flower that catches your eye.

And why not? You're a grown up now. No one, *no one* is going to say no to you. So go nuts; but know that you may have to hang up that smock when you get to the nursery. It'll only get in the way.

Reason #2:

<u>Like The Cleaning Of A House ...</u>

... Gardening never ends. And you wouldn't carve a pastime out of housecleaning, now would you? Wait, *would you*? Perhaps I have misjudged the breadth of my readers' ... er, quirkiness. Any mopping enthusiasts out there? Closet dusting fanatics? Closet ... closet organizers? Weirdos, the lot of you. Maybe you deserve a go at gardening. You know, whenever you're done vacuuming.

Now, I suppose it is true that any hobby worth its salt should not *end* per se—the attraction of such recreational pursuits lies in one's ability to continue pursuing them, after all. But whereas most other hobbies allow the hobbyist to engage and disengage at will (Attention everybody: I have picked up my knitting needles; I am now knitting; I will continue to knit for the remainder of this recreational interlude, at which point I will set down my knitting needles; then, although I will no longer be knitting, I will remain, in spirit, a *knitteur*), a garden does not sit idly by whenever you drop the rake. It does not collect dust on a shelf when you do not have time to attend to it. It cannot be set aside when the phone rings, to be picked up and resumed once you return and find your place. A garden is not readily boxed-up and shoved into the crawlspace when you outgrow it and move on to other interests (well, perhaps *Dahlia* tubers and the like could hunker down in the attic for a while, but by and large crawlspaces do not present an ideal exposure for most plants). Nor can the garden be held at some safe remove, like the ski slopes or the swimming pool, to be sought out and traveled to at times of official hobby engagement and then left behind as someone else's concern when you've had enough moguls or high-dives for one day.

No, a garden lurks right outside the window, reminding you around the clock that it is, by your grace and whimsy, alive. All day, all year long, it is persistently growing, changing and demanding the water, energy, and attention that are the birthright of all living things. When these pestering demands are not met, say when you are out of town for the weekend, or when you decide you'd like to try—I don't know—macrame, or basejumping, or *anything* at all else for a couple weeks, then the garden sulks, pouts, wilts, and is overrun with opportunistic pestilence. It languishes. It ceases to be a garden and reverts instead to some snarling, feral, pre-horticultural state until such a time as it can be tamed once more.

For those who are foolish enough to engage the garden in this unhealthy, codependent relationship, all notions of eventual completion, closure, or end-product must be systematically eradicated from the mind. In the garden, moving on to the next thing does not signal any real accomplishment or victory, but at best some unsteady truce between yourself and the previous thing, riddled with cynicism and a mutual expectation that one or the other of you will inevitably violate the terms of your agreement. And this is why gardening never ends. There is no experiential or material culmination of your toil that is not soon riven by the opposing wills of gardener and garden. A pruned shrub does not cease to grow. A weeded bed is a vacuum into which the next generation of weeds is already launching its coup. In pruning, in weeding, you did not finish anything—and you never will.

For unlike, say, knitting, gardening does not result in any finished product. The garden is no knit blanket to be completed and passed down between generations marked only by the loving and careworn touch of time. If a garden *were* like a blanket—oh, where shall we begin—it would suffer a continuous and weekly unraveling; it would become overrun with lice in the summer warmth; it would need to be carefully soaked every couple days lest it shrivel and, cruelly desiccated, crumble into dust. Yes, neighborhood birds, squirrels and deer would sneak into the living room at night and munch on the woolen yarn leaving you with nothing but tatters by morning. Random knots would spring up across the face of the blanket, snarling the delicate pattern until it could be fastidiously untangled, *during* which disentangling, other knots would doubtless have sprung up elsewhere. Whole sections of the accursed blanket would—if it were truly gardenly—just turn brown and rot away. Was it a fungus? bacteria? perhaps it was viral—you just never know! And anyway it doesn't matter because by this point there's a more pressing issue to deal with: the blanket is growing. Rapidly. In no time, the careful square shaped by your grandmother's knitting needle has ballooned out into some ragged, organic form to smother the leather recliner over which it once draped, folded, so neatly. Before your eyes, it reaches out to envelop the sofa as well. Your attempts to head back this living room insurrection by bundling up the blanket and tossing it outside works for a moment, but before long, you notice, dozens of little offshoot baby blankets have popped up from bits of yarn left behind. You only made things worse. And that's when you realize: that fool grandma of yours knit some kind of invasive blanket.

A terrifying thought, certainly. But a bit surreal. To better approximate the unique and ceaseless attention demanded by a garden, we should perhaps turn to a different analogy—something alive, something harebrained, something every bit as ridiculous and masochistic as the gardener's chosen lot. Wait—I've got it! If anything, tending a garden is more like … running a petting zoo … in your backyard … as a hobby.

Yes, a petting zoo. Now, it would be one thing if you decided to try your hand at running a petting zoo as a career.

You could charge admission, let neighborhood kids feed the animals—five bucks for a picture with the alpaca—that sort of thing. Your business acumen may be called into question, but it would at least be a way to justify the inordinate amount of time and money required to keep so many living things alive and happy in your backyard.

But oh, no, this is no professional endeavor. You are not even afforded whatever paltry benefit of the doubt is reserved for the downtrodden entrepreneur. That's because, in this case, you've got sheep, goats, pot-bellied pigs, turkeys, a pony, ferrets, guinea pigs, rabbits, and a surly llama out there jostling for space, getting diseases, attracting coyotes, eating, shedding, and fighting—all for fun. Or to satisfy some creative urge, or to connect with nature, or maybe lower (!) your stress or something. Who knows. Like with gardening, people on the outside can't really fathom why you do it.

And the worst part is that, rather than confront or reign in the lunacy of your hobby, you just keep adding to it. You willingly propagate the chaos. You set the plates spinning and immediately look for more. Why, just last weekend you bought a dozen messenger pigeons, from a mail-order catalog, to add to your madcap petting zoo. I ask you: who in the world wants to pet a pigeon?

Well, who in the world wants to prune a rose? Who wants to pull horsetails? Who in the world wants to remove dogwood suckers again? It is not that gardeners *want* to do these things (though some will claim they do), but unless we learn to derive at least some satisfaction from such small, repetitive, and seemingly insignificant tasks as these, the never-ending whirl and madness of gardening would quickly slap us down in a rush of headlong futility.

And now that I see it spelled out like that, I find myself more favorably considering the petting-zoo scenario. Or housecleaning, for that matter. At least the vacuum is housebroken.

Reason #3:

The Case Of Michael R. Clancy-Dubuquesne McGumbyton III

Do you have a hard time remembering people's names? Coworkers, friends of friends, nieces and nephews, B-list actors, municipal political candidates—do they all just sort of jumble together into a loose pile of stock first names and mostly fabricated surnames? Does it seem like you know a lot of Patricias even though you can't come up with any on the spot?

Well, then, gardening may not be for you.

You see, plant names are just like our own—only with more rules, and more flagrant disregard for those rules. Oh, and with greater use of dead languages. And so many syllables. Also, the names change pretty often. And they're different from place to—

—Tell you what, there's actually a lot of ways that plant names are different from people names, and they're all pretty obnoxious. Rather than belabor these with painful enumeration, I'll try to transpose them into a more familiar context. Which I will then belabor anyway, but in a more amusing way.

Ready? Too bad, here we go.

Let's say you have a colleague named Mike. At least you call him Mike. You seem to recall him telling you his full name was something highfalutin and cumbersome like Michael R. Clancy-Dubuquesne McGumbyton … uh, III. That's probably not quite right, but let's face it, there's no way you're going to remember the whole thing. It may as well be Latin. You're reasonably confident in the "Mike" part, anyway.

And "Mike" suffices for nomenclature—oh, most of the time. The only problem comes at the office (did I mention you work in an office?) where there are at least four other guys named Mike. Now, each Mike works in a different department, so the issue arises primarily at bigger meetings, social events, and such, whereupon the shouting of "Mike!"

could be expected to draw no fewer than five turned heads in response.

To remedy this dilemma, each department, being vaguely aware that there are more Mikes out there in the great wide office, comes up with a more descriptive, personalized nickname for its respective Mike. Within his own corner of the office, a given Mike may be identified by reference to an inside joke, a habitual quirk or some puzzling non-sequiteur. So maybe there's Waterslide Mike, Jäger Mike, Mike-rophone, General MikeCarther, and—I don't know— "Wooky".

Unfortunately, these local nicknames are not well-known outside each department. Your department doesn't know that "Jäger Mike" is the nom de guerre of Mike over in Accounting. Rather, you've all come up with your *own* taxonomy for use in referring to inter-departmental Mikes. For example, your close colleague Mike McGumbyton goes by "Mike-rophone" in your neck of the cubicle woods (he's a regular on the happy-hour karaoke circuit) but when any other Mike comes up in conversation, your department uses a nickname that more closely links him to his official responsibilities, thus "Mike in Accounting" becomes "Math

Mike", the one in Marketing is "Mad Mike" (like "Mad Men", get it?), and so on and so on. *Every department in the building is doing this for every Mike in the building.*

Are you keeping track? How many different handles is that for each Mike? Somewhere in the neighborhood of 5-10, depending on how many departments there are in your office. And we're only getting started.

To further muddle the Mike-scape, one nickname might refer to more than one Mike. Perhaps Accounting calls your own Mike (aka Mike McGumbyton; aka Mike-rophone) "Mad Mike" because he's given to petulance when no one wants to come karaoke-ing after work on Thursdays. Now two different Mikes have been silly-puttied into the same entity. This is just dangerous! Already, it has led to several instances of misapplied gossip and at least one case of the wrong Mike being invited to join a fantasy football league. Everyone knows "Mad" (as in angry) Mike (Mcgumbyton) [the Mike-rophone] has no time for sports; he's a karaoke man, and as such would rather sing along to Nickleback than talk quarterbacks. It should also be noted that due to a preternatural stubborn streak within your office, each department insists, to the brink of physical violence, that they have correctly applied the name "Mad Mike", and damned if either side is going to give in.

And it gets worse. Because certain of these local aliases inevitably spread through the office to catch on in departments other than their origin—with varying degrees of accuracy. By now, for example, everyone has heard of "Wookie" and is pretty sure that it refers to one of the Mikes. But since "Wookie" contains, at best, ambiguous character description, it's anyone's guess which Mike is the true "Wookie". The Mike in HR (alternately "*H*igh *R*oller Mike", "Nice Mike", or "The Shrink") is pretty hairy, perhaps *he's* "Wookie". Or wait—the Mike over in Testing (oh, jeez, he's probably aka "Mike-check", "McStress-Test" and "Mike-otic", to name a few) is pretty tall, does that make *him* Wookie? Or maybe, a la the "Mad Mike" fiasco, they *both* are "Wookie". Then again, it could be the case that "Wookie" is someone who doesn't even work at the office. Maybe "Wookie" is not a person at all, but rather a code word for a popular but quasi-legal extracurricular activity engaged in by some of the more duplicitous characters on staff (probably something like street-racing suped-up bumper cars—but I wouldn't know anything about that). Or, maybe, there are just a lot of Star Wars conversations going on around the water cooler.

At a certain point, fed up with the snafus, miscommunication, and knife fights, office management steps in. They decide they're going to settle things once and for all. (One manager, in particular, is tired of fielding nonsensical fantasy football trade offers from a Mike who never should have been in the league to begin with.) Their solution: a sweeping mandate to use full names around the office. And not just for Mikes, since that would smack of discrimination. Every. Single. Employee. Must now be recognized by their complete name—however replete with titles, accents, hyphens, or poorly anglicized spellings. This is, after all, the only *correct*, fair, and unambiguous way to classify people.

Well, a few sycophants give it a shot. They spend late evenings pouring over the employee contact spreadsheet management sent out, committing as many names to memory as possible. Some are pretty easy; it turns out one of the Mikes is just Mike Jones—how much simpler would that have been? The worst brown-nosers go so far as to memorize a few of the longest, trickiest names just to show off. One exceptional jackass makes a point of greeting the receptionist every morning, at nearly a shout: "Why, if it isn't Jacqueline D'æphçréenñğschtsksk Östergroot-Smythe! Beautiful morning, wouldn't you say?" (The guy must have been a linguistics major or something.) But for the most part, names are just butchered and half-assed and mangled and misapplied all over the place.

One unforeseen consequence of such reckless appellation is that some employees begin to feel alienated from their given and family names. Such persistent confrontation with their ungainly shape and sound in coworkers' clumsy mouths has rendered them meaningless and false. These individuals cease responding to their legal names and, in a crisis of identity, begin to suspect shenanigans somewhere in their family tree: adoption, inbreeding, kidnapping—those sorts of things.

The only path to true peace of mind, obviously, is genetic testing. Now, at first, only the most distraught and angst-ridden workers go this route, but once a few folks are seen swabbing and collecting DNA samples to send in to the lab, nearly everyone feels compelled to join in, to play their part in straightening out this mess of nomenclature and phylogeny.

And right about here is where the wheels fall off—or rather, a few weeks later, when a flood of test results inundate your (now hapless and wholly unproductive) office.

Because as it turns out, almost no one is who they thought they were. The genetic test results indicate that nearly every employee has been incorrectly claimed and named by a family that does not match his/her DNA. How one company ended up with so many misfit bastards and orphans is truly a mystery, but needless to say, the revelation results in a flurry of sudden name changes over the weekend. Some of your coworkers reclaim the proud heritage of a long lost family crest; some see an opportunity to start afresh with a new, unsullied name; some decide to keep their cumbersome, misleading surname as a tribute to their past, but go on and change their first name anyway because, well, everyone else is doing it. It's possible, after all is said and done, there may actually be a few *more* Mikes than when we started.

And now no one knows what the hell to call anyone else. Your whole office is gobstruck and tongue-tied, reduced to grunts and gestures. Fragments of names old and new flit about the cubicles, not knowing whom to settle upon. Management is sacked for their hand in the mess, although many of these go on working since ownership no longer has any idea how to locate, much less give notice to, any specific individual in their employ. All day, hollow nobodies bump about the office, robbed of their identity. Now and then, perhaps whispered under the breath, can be heard a plaintive refrain of "*Mike?*" from over the cubicle walls—this, a quivering, unanswered plea for simpler times.

And that is the parable of how plants get their names. Step into the office of gardening and you'll be soon be yearning for a time when you had the presence and clarity of mind to consider which, if any, of your eight nieces was named Patricia.

Reason #4

<u>Pop The Trunk</u>

I'm sorry, but before we get any further into this discourse, we're going to need to establish whether or not you have the necessary infrastructure in place for a successful foray into horticulture. The more you can plan and be prepared for some of the common logistical challenges you are likely to face, the more smoothly this transition will go. So, first things first, if I may—what kind of truck do you drive?

...

What? Why are you looking at me like that? I know the question might seem forward—we only just met, after all —but let me remind you, you're the one thinking about becoming a gardener. I am merely doing what I can to mitigate your questionable life choices. You're welcome. That being said, the question remains. What kind of truck do you drive?

...

Wait, wait, wait—what do you mean, you don't *have* a truck? That's not even—look, do you want to be a gardener or not? You haven't thought this through at all, have you? Ba! You're just like the rest. You think you become a gardener and overnight *poof!*— plants and tools and mulch and soil and trellises and arbors and pots and edging and flagstones and tumbling compost bins and ladders and kitschy plastic yard art and lumber and paver-sand and sundials and birdbaths and fleece vests just magically appear in your driveway? You think you start ripping out sod and weeds and stumps and dead lilacs and fenceposts and that brick path you keep tripping on and that creepy shed that might be haunted and *bingo bango!*—the good gardening fairy swoops in while your back is turned to spirit your trash piles away to the dump? Why are you snickering? You don't think the good gardening fairy says "*bingo bango*"? Of course she does! That does it. If you can't take this seriously, I'm going to go write cautionary nonfiction for someone else!

...

<*Sigh*> Okay, sorry I snapped there. It's been a long day and I'm running out of coffee. I'll try to walk you through it. Gardening, more than most other hobbies/lifestyles/cults involves a lot of logistics. It is, at its very core, an exercise in inefficiency. While the net gain of your activity is measured in vague increments of aesthetic surplus and existential affirmation, the gross inflow and outflow of materials is colossal and does not look good on paper. This soil is bad, haul it away and bring in new soil; that's good, but it needs manure, someone go get chicken manure; these plants are bad, dig them up, haul them away and bring in new ones; there should be more rocks here; this topology is all wrong, *this* hill should be over *there*; we need a new hill! Why are there so many rocks here?

It is a steady influx of dirty, heavy, and awkward materials, which are often living or otherwise prohibitively fragile in nature. The bulk of the efflux is more of the same, though quite often less alive and fragile after passing through the meat-grinder of your care. (Not pointing fingers, just saying; get used to it.)

The bottom line is: you're going to need a truck for all

this stuff. Every gardener has a truck, even if they won't admit it. Myself, I favor the older models. Tried and true, they don't make 'em like they used to and all that. My 1996 Honda Civic hatchback has been with me through thick and thin and I wouldn't—

...

What's that? A Honda Civic—you've never heard of a Civic? How is that possible?

...

What do you mean, it's not a truck? Oh—Okay, I see what's happening here. You're one of those people who hears "truck" and sees a gleaming juggernaut as big and expensive as a small house—a house-truck, right? A country rock anthem breaks out while a rumbly-voiced narrator hawks up engineering superlatives like so much phlegm. V8 engines and torque and steel—is that what you're thinking when I say "truck"? Gravel and chains. Leather gloves. You want to talk payload and bed-liners and suspension; you want to take a look under the hood, don't you?

Well, you can pop hoods and rev engines all you like, but when it comes to evaluating appropriate gardening trucks, I'd rather you pop the trunk. Because no matter your conveyance, whatever get-up you are currently driving, riding, pedaling, or pushing, can and will become your truck. Such is the gardener's lot. If it can carry a single seed or trowel, it is a truck as far as I'm concerned. If you're willing to compromise the safety of passengers and driver alike by cramming in a piece of rusty scrap metal to decorate the perennial bed, you've got a truck. And if you're willing to bury its resale value under a layer of spilled bark mulch, fertilizer and potting soil, you've found yourself a truck, my friend. If it smells like fish meal, I'm sorry to say, it's a truck.

This philosophy is one born of frugality and necessity. There's no denying the bald-eagle-soaring, diesel-rattling, gravel-crunching awesomeness of a traditional house-truck—I drove one such beast for years at work and would not hesitate to belt out a twangy anthem in its defense —but since I can't afford to buy one of my own, and since I have not been blessed with a particularly anthemic voice, I have been forced to re-evaluate the whole "truck" archetype. And if I have, then so should you.

Good, I'm glad we're in agreement.

The way I/we look at it is like this: for whatever reason, many people who purchase house-trucks do not choose to unleash their vehicle's raw, essential "truckness" to get work done. These curious sorts can often be found at your local garden center, asking an employee to put down garbage bags in the bed of their beautiful behemoth before carefully loading a flat of geraniums in such a way as to minimize undue spillage of potting soil/leaf debris, etc.

Such is the prerogative of the house-truck owner, but if you happen to represent such a demographic, may I pose a couple of questions: 1.) Why do you? and 2.) Can I borrow your truck?

More often amongst gardeners, it is the case that folks find themselves with a truck-worthy project at hand, but—alas!—no truck in sight. And wouldn't you know it, most people within this unfortunate bracket seem to have somehow misplaced the $50,000 or so they usually keep tucked away for precisely this sort of contingency. Unwilling to abandon their dreams of raised beds and pergolas, they are then forced to seek truckness elsewhere. It is under such duress that everyday objects possessed of even the most primitive mobility get press-ganged into truck duty. Don't let anyone tell you you can't drag a painter's tarp full of free wood chips across the neighborhood from an arborist's jobsite. Where there is a will, and a fool, there is a way. Soon you, too, will find yourself seeing trucks wherever your gaze lingers. Because whether by Kia, rickshaw or mule—one way or another, you've got to get your marigolds from point A to point B.

So pop the trunk; let's see what you've got.

…

Ah, what have we here? Looks like a minivan-truck. Those are great, a lot of length to work with. You could fit a whole tree in there. Maybe two or three. Wanna try? Okay, maybe later.

And what's this? A sedan-truck? Leather seats? Throw down a tarp and you're good to go. You could shuttle a whole squad of garden gnomes, easy. Careful though; those guys can get … unruly in groups.

Ah yes, I already mentioned the hatchback-truck, my personal favorite. Admittedly, I'm a bit biased, but just try it —there's nothing you can't fit in one of these. The rototiller was a close call, but I'd rather have a rototiller than a passenger seat, any day.

You're wondering about a public transportation-truck? Yeah, that's a thing. I once had a gardener coworker who would commute to the jobsite by city bus—she'd just bundle up all her rakes and spades and whatnot and sling 'em over her shoulder like a badass garden quiver. (I thought it was badass, anyway.)

Oh, lets see, what else do we have here … a moped-truck? That works too: one flat of pansies on the floorboard and a roll of weed-barrier on your lap. Bingo, bango.

Bicycle-truck? Hey, those little pull-along trailers aren't just for babies anymore. I'm thinking a quarter-yard of compost if you're a strong pedaler. You may want to hose it down before baby's next ride, though.

Skateboard truck? Well that's easy, a skateboard is basically a small dolly. Here—give me a hand with this bird bath.

Whoa, whoa, whoa—what's this? A Canoe-truck? You've got a canoe-truck? Well, Okay, that's a little weird. But still, there's clearly storage to be had. Didn't people use to travel out West in canoes? Sure—I bet you could do a whole rockery in less than three trips.

Wait a minute, did you come *here* in a canoe? Seriously—who are you people? You know what, forget it, I don't even want to know. I'm out of here. I don't have time for this kind of crazy—I've got a load of chicken manure to put in the trunk of my truck.

...

So, hey, I'm back. If, uh—boy I hate to ask this, especially now—but seriously, if any of you out there has a real truck, can I ... borrow it? Just for the afternoon? Please? This chicken manure is pretty rank.

Reason #5

<u>Gold-Digger</u>

Get out your purse. Get out your wallet. Check your balances. Clean and oil your credit cards. Raid your piggy bank. Raid your daughter's piggy bank and tell yourself it's really *your* money until she turns eighteen. Take out a loan. Misappropriate an existing loan. Re-allocate funds earmarked for utilities. Re-allocate coins earmarked for the laundromat. Take a liberal view of budgetary categories. Fudge the numbers. Pawn a set of heirloom cufflinks. Go without luxuries like food and socks. Consider busking. Consider a life of petty crime.

You've got a new mouth to feed.

Voracious and flirty, needy, nubile, cunning and coy —this one's a gold-digger. And it pegged you for a sucker from the start. There you were, maybe dragged out on some boring garden tour with a friend, wishing you were back home with your jigsaw puzzles, when this hot new hobby caught your eye with a stargazer lily. You gawked and drooled; the garden sensed you, lonely and gullible, and doubled down.

Now here you are at the altar with that cute green thing, sporting your finest fleece vest, some ridiculous hat or other, clogs, and rose-pruning gauntlets. Your garden-to-be says you look good like that. You don't.

You stumble through your vows—some drivel about weeding in any weather; planting come rain or shine—and then it's time to commit. I'd think long and hard, if I were you. Because as soon as you say *I do* it's all over. The check is cashed; the bank is broken. From now on you're nothing but a sugar mama/daddy as long as that hussy garden can flash a bare patch of soil or bat its witch-hazel lashes, begging for more. More finery, more foliage, more flowers; more time, more lovin' … and more money. Always more money.

First come the plants.

Whatever catches your eye, darling, nothing's too

good for my baby, you'll swoon.

Nothing? Not even Japanese maples at a few hundred bucks a pop? How about slow-growing, contorted shrubs marked up by the inch? Late night, impulsive orders to pricey seed catalogs? Woodland ephemerals as expensive and hard to pronounce as obscure gemstones? Two-hundred-pound Cat-buddha statues? Whole drifts of trendy perennials with trademarked names all permutated from the same half-dozen adjectives and nouns?

How much for five flats of 'Limelight Frostbeam Splendor' Heuchera? You won't ask, because it doesn't matter. The little garden gets what it wants.

Soon, they'll start to recognize you down at the garden center. At first it's kind of cute. You're so blind and in love—skipping up and down the aisles; throwing plants in the cart which don't have a shot in hell of surviving; coming back for more when those die; hemorrhaging money with each visit. Anything to make your garden happy—it is happy, isn't it?

But once the honeymoon wears off, your bank accounts begin to sputter. Your checks bounce. Soon, your credit cards are rejected on sight. The look on the garden center employees' face says this is getting less cute.

With your coffers drained and credit shot, but your leafy concubine demanding ever more attention, you dig deep and try some thrifty gardening. This involves any number of quasi-legal techniques which lean heavily on a subjective interpretation of "found" versus "stolen" materials. No one's going to miss a few seeds, a few cuttings, a few dozen bricks left near enough the street to suggest (albeit not with specific signage) a "free pile". You begin to clutter up your once vestal garden with salvaged items slated for "repurposing", although to what new purpose or from which old, remains something of a mystery. Mostly, it just stays junk.

The garden-love does not appreciate this sort of treatment. It has clear expectations of your relationship together and you are failing to meet them. It pouts and rejects your penny-pinching and is surly. Seeds don't germinate; cuttings don't take. Neighbors pound on the door at all hours demanding their property back. (In your defense, that wheelbarrow was parked pretty darn close to the trash bins). The city proclaims your garden-turned-scrap-heap an eyesore. Your once blushing betrothed is now turning red for all the wrong reasons. In short, it is not much fun to be around.

You need something to rekindle that elusive spark—perhaps to convince yourself there ever was a spark to begin with. What you need is a grand gesture, a bold statement in that timeless idiom of romance—you need a Big Purchase.

Never mind how you'll pay for it. Rest assured, where there's a broken relationship, there's a dollar for duct tape. (I'll refer you back to the top of this section if you're short on ideas.) The more important question is what to buy.

You'll have to look beyond plants at this point. You need something that will let you spend some real quality time with your garden—either that, or something to assuage the guilt of enjoying each other's absence. Tools are a good start, but by now you will have already bought any number of saws, pruners and gadgety weeding tools, hoping to create magic. You will have already resorted to powered hedge trimmers, chainsaws, leaf blowers, rototillers, line trimmers and the like to get some attention—all to no avail. Oh, perhaps somewhere along the way, a golden afternoon was had, coughing and sputtering in two-stroke engine bliss—but those toys soon went the way of all fancy: spurned and then forgotten, in dust, in shame.

What you really need is something to symbolize the raw, hydraulic power of your love and devotion; something that says you will move the very heavens and earth for your precious little garden. Something that—wait, that's it! Move the earth! You need a tractor! A backhoe! A front-loader! A skid-steer! Some massive piece of machinery to unearth your feelings for each other.

And here is where I'll leave you to your fate. For you know as well as I do that anything bigger than a push-mower and a shovel will be utterly wasted on your $1/10^{th}$ acre lot. You know such an extravagant metal beast will only turn to rust, unused, and become nothing but the steel elephant in the room of your garden marriage. You know this, but it is quite likely you have already run off to some tractor showcase at the nearest state fair.

So, since you're clearly in no state to heed wisdom, let me just say to an empty room and posterity: a garden will never be sated. Plants, tools, imported clogs, a backhoe—it does not matter *what* you spend money on, only that you continue to do so for as long as you both shall live. Whatever your tax-bracket, no matter the size of your yard, all a simple

gold-digging garden ever wanted was to take all your money
—and break your heart.

Reason #6

Name ... That ... Plant!

Laaadies and Gentlemen! Gardeners and garden-nerds! Garden-his and Garden-hers! Green and black-thumbs alike, welcome to another episode of ... NAME ... THAT ... PLANT!!!!

Okay, look at me—eyes right here: you can do this. I know it's a ridiculous show, but if you're going to be a gardener you have to get through this sooner or later. We've all been contestants at some point. Do you want to stretch out, maybe? Warm up or something? Here, let's run through some South-African perennials real quick. No? Okay, I respect that; you just want to get in the zone. That's fine. Try to go zen, whatever works for you.

That's right, it's no one's favorite gardening quiz

show where reluctant contestants field nonsensical questions
from audience members who couldn't tell a flower from flank
steak, a tree from a tire-iron, or a plant from a pair of pants!
What! The! Heck! are these people talking about!?

<Weak applause>

Now, let's bring out our first contestant!

All right, they're looking at you. Go on, get up there.
Good luck! And don't worry, I'll be right here to help you.
Now stay sharp, the first question is always tough. By which
I mean impossible. Just kidding. Not really—not really
kidding. It's impossible.

Let's get started, shall we? First question. This one
comes from a random, online acquaintance with whom you
may or may not actually be acquainted. He has bumped into
you on the street and must have heard that you were, like,
into plants and stuff. And I quote: "Dude, this one plant I
saw, s'got these green leaves like ... that? Uh, I think it had
flowers, maybe—wait, unless those are the leaves—but it's
about yay big <makes vague gesture with one arm,
constrained by no discernible frame of reference>" ...

Wow! Now that is a doozy of a ... question? Was that
even a question, folks? In any case, how do you respond,

contestant number one?

Okay, like I said, there's no way you're going to get this one, and it doesn't matter because there's no way that guy would know *if* you got the right answer. My advice would be to come in fast with some heavy Latin and then hedge your bets with a really generic sounding plant that can't possibly be correct. Keep 'em off balance. Project confidence.

" … Er, uh … yeah, the uh, the plant in question is likely a *Viburnum plicatum f. tomentosum* 'Marriesii'. Either that, or a … cactus. Yeah, I'm going to go with a cactus."

Bravo, you are a natural at this. Pedantic *and* smart ass, I couldn't have answered better myself.

Contestant number one has responded with 'a cactus' … and the correct answer is: no one knows! There's not a person alive who can tell what this guy's talking about! It could be a Caryopteris, could be a carrot! Either way, he's pretty sure you're wrong. Moving on to question two—

You're hanging in there so far. Stay on your toes though, the second question usually hits close to home.

—and this next question comes from … contestant number one's very own mother!

Yikes. Close to home, indeed.

49

Okay, question number two, from dear old Mom: "Honey, what are those flowers I'm seeing everywhere right now"?

Boy, sorry honey, you're on your own for this one. All I can tell you is that family members, especially parents, like to think of you as an expert in whatever it is you do, so try to play to that. You just have to convince *her*.

"Um. Hi … Mom. Yeah, that's uh … that's *Forsythia* you're seeing everywhere."

Argh, you fool! It's August, no one will believe it's *Forsythia* blooming now!

Aaaaand, according to mother-dearest, "For-Cynthia" is correct! She told all her friends you would know the answer and, furthermore, she's very proud of you and what you've done with your life!

Wow, I stand corrected. You have a very … nice mother.

Now we move on to question number three—
<DING DING DING!>
Uh oh.
—ohhooh! And you all know what that bell means: question number three will be a 'whatsthis' question! That's

right, one of our audience members has brought with him, in his pocket, a small sample of mangled, long-dead plant material he would like you to identify. This, he will unceremoniously shove in your face and say ... 'whatsthis'!?

And here we have our audience member—yes, hello sir, you're looking displeased today—and he is producing the sample ... and there we have it—what looks to be a challenging mystery, from an unpleasant man. So, contestant number one, we ask you ... whatsthis?

Ugh, that doesn't look good. Looks like it's been in that guy's pocket since last month. Is that a leaf or part of an old sandwich? Well, your guess is as good as mine. Unfortunately, these types of people are usually the hardest to satisfy.

Contestant number one, we await your response.

"Oh, wow. Okay. That looks like it might have been a *Bergenia* or … a piece of lettuce?"

Ohh! Wrong answer! Our audience member is not amused. No sir, he does not share your sense of humor. Furthermore, he would like to know what kind of idiots we get on this show! Simple, my dear audience member: we get gardeners.

Well, that was a cheap shot.

Now, for the fourth and final question ...

Okay, the fourth question always has some important piece of information they leave out until the very end. Just stay sharp; you have to be patient.

For the final question, we head down to the local garden center. This customer here is looking for suggestions on what plant to buy for a very ... specific ... spot. Hello ma'am, are you ready to confound our contestant? Wonderful, she has no idea what we're talking about. Aaaand ... go!

...

Psst! That's your cue! You have to prompt the customer. Like, figure out a plant that will work for her.

"Oh! Uh, Okay. Well, ma'am, why don't you tell me about the spot where you're going to be putting this plant."

There you go, champ.

"Oh, I don't know. It gets some light there, but not a ton."

"I ... see. And, do you want ... flowers? Orrr, something evergreen ... what?"

"Flowers would be nice. Doesn't have to have

flowers, though."

"Hmm. Well, are there any plants you know you like, or don't like?"

"Oh, you know, nothing sharp or pokey. Nothing like a pine tree, I hate pine trees—"

Psst! Me again. Here's a hint, when she says she hates "pine trees", that could mean anything. She has no idea what a pine tree is, trust me. If you show her a hemlock, she'll think it's a pine tree. If you show her a heather, she'll think it's a pine tree. She's claiming her right to refuse any plant you suggest based on its perceived or imagined kinship to a "pine tree". That's all—carry on.

"—but I do love old-fashioned roses."

Yeah, like those aren't "pokey".

"Okay, um, well how big of a space do you have to work with?"

"Not too big, I suppose. Maybe a couple feet."

"A couple feet … wide, or tall, or … ?"

"Well, obviously it can't be too tall."

Obviously.

"What's the soil like, there?"

"You know, I'd use regular soil."

"You'd … use … regular—okay, well, how about water, is it a wet spot, or dry? Does it get rain? Is there irrigation?"

<Gives funny look> "Well, I would water it, of course."

See the way she answered that? Something's not right here. She's leaving something out, I can feel it.

"Well … that gives you quite a few options. You said it gets some light, what's the exposure? North side of the house? South side?"

<Frowns in concentration> "Kind of in the middle, I guess."

" … In the middle? The middle of what?"

Haha! Oh, here it comes.

"Well, it's by the couch, pretty much the middle of the living room."

Bam! Oh, that's a classic. Wanted an indoor plant, but didn't tell you until the end. Ha! You should have given her the old-fashioned rose! Look, I'm sorry, I was lying when I said I'd be here to help you. There is no help in this game. You just lose.

<BUZZER SOUNDS>

Oh, I'm sorry, contestant one, it looks like we've run out of time! On behalf of our audience, I'd like to thank you for playing. Unfortunately, you didn't win tonight, but if it's any consolation, no one ever does! We'll see you next time (and there will certainly be a next time), and remember: no matter how well you know plants, you never know enough to ... NAME ... THAT ... PLANT!

<Half-hearted applause, a smattering of boos>

I hate this show.

Reason #7

The Asylum

But what of the satisfaction? you may be asking.
Where is that warm glow of accomplishment long spoken of
at length and with little provocation by gardeners
everywhere, even when told repeatedly to shut-up about it?
A fair question. To be sure, gardening has its share of
small victories, chest-thumping triumphs, and even the
occasional full-choir, golden hallelujah. Such moments are
indeed rewarding and fulfilling and all those other fuzzy,
smug sensations to boot. But the reason gardeners won't shut-
up about them is not because they feel so good; it's because,
really, no one else cares. And that drives us kind of crazy.

By way of example, let's look at a particularly
beloved gardening task: pruning (no, I'm not kidding, we

love this stuff). A good pruning job, as with many of gardening's rapturous, ultimately meaningless achievements, is its own reward. It has to be.

Imagine yourself in a serious, dormant-season pruning session. You've been going around the yard addressing all your deciduous trees like a door-to-door salesman, convincing each one its life would be so much more fantastic if you were only allowed to come in for a minute. Today you've been working the maples. Good work. Really, in my opinion some very lovely pruning you've done there. But then, I'm a gardener. Unfortunately, I am also the narrator, and as such it falls to me to give you the—rather less flattering—perspective from which you will be seen by the rest of the non-gardening world. You know that Japanese Maple that you just spent all afternoon working on—part surgeon, part sculptor, part biologist, part craftsman, and part parent? The one you eyeballed and squinted at and stepped back from and paced around and sized up and talked to and frowned at and approached and stepped back from again for the better part of an hour before you even dared brandish pruners? The sad truth is that the overwhelming majority of people in this world will never appreciate what you have accomplished with that tree. What's worse, many among this faction will push right past indifference to frank distrust and resentment of the time and effort you put into such a futile task. They would feel better if you were perhaps looked after and occasionally medicated in a devoted facility for the horticulturally afflicted. They think you are mad.

It certainly doesn't help dispel such sentiments that, in an effort to correctly time your pruning with the tree's dormancy, you have chosen the dead of Winter to put on your show of gardening lunacy.

And while such misunderstood branding may place you, in your own addled mind, in the company of other persecuted geniuses who trod the line between madness and brilliance, this is, unfortunately, not the sort of madness they mean. At very best, in their esteem, you could hope to be written off as some sort of Eccentric Artist Lite, with trees and shrubs as your unfortunate media, and naught but chittering squirrels as your audience. You may as well be scrap-booking, on top of a ladder, in Winter, for all to see.

It can be disheartening, to say the least. For while you may swell with fragile pride to see your correctly angled and well-placed thinning cuts healing over well, while you may sigh with relief that your necessary few heading cuts did not sucker too horribly, and while your own breath may come easier in direct correlation to the freer circulation about the previously congested interior of the tree, these feelings are gobbledygook to the world at large, so don't bother trying to convey them to anyone but your therapist. Even then, use discretion: there is a special place for people like you.

Make no mistake—your work, though meticulous and precise, is also arcane. It is a practice born of discipline, experience, artistry, and some sort of chemical imbalance. It is akin to a sublime and not especially enthralling circus act. Do not be surprised when paying spectators request a refund.

To the trained eye, a well-pruned plant is a thing of calm beauty, free of the subconscious tension wrought by crossing branches, dead wood, and subtle, insidious disease. There is a give and take. There is communication. There is grace.

But how many trained eyes do you know?

To the layman, over whose head these subtle visual affirmations will *whoosh* like a flock of starlings, the results of your careful skill are stuck at the far end of a tenuous cause/effect relationship that involves the plant *not* doing something—namely, not dying. It is a bold (and, let's face it, not very impressive) claim to point out your Japanese Maple to a skeptical neighbor and insist that its apparent good health and relative vitality is a direct result of your cryptic winter shenanigans.

"Congratulations," he/she will mutter, "your tree is alive". *And your car didn't blow up on the drive home; that doesn't make you a great mechanic.*

So many of our goals in pruning are long term and preventative, that it can be difficult to rationalize our actions to friends and family, much less to peers or complete strangers. The best way (though still not a good way) to do so is to call attention to the barbaric pruning habits of others. For it is only at the hands of the reckless, the impatient, and the apathetic that good pruning may achieve some sort of validation-by-contrast. Take note, for example, of the cruel abandon with which they hack back their shrubs every year. Then, later on, feel free to indulge a small, bitter smile when their hydrangeas fail utterly to bloom. Explain to passers by why these hydrangeas have failed utterly to bloom. Pretend their sad shakes of the head as they walk away are directed toward the unfulfilled hydrangea potential and not toward your own downward spiral. This will be your only consolation, and it is an unsatisfying, petty one.

You may attempt, instead, to graciously walk over and offer a word of advice on proper timing for pruning shrubs that bloom on old wood. Just a helpful tidbit of neighborly wisdom. Because who *doesn't* appreciate unsolicited advice from the weirdo across the street? Even presuming the best of intentions, your words will likely fall on deaf ears. Your neighbor has bigger concerns—namely, your very presence in their yard constitutes an exposure to the threat of contagious garden crazy. That stuff is spreading. Why, your ridiculous hat alone must be *lousy* with untold horti-cooties. At the mere mention of "pruning" they will bristle and cover their mouths. They are not "pruning", they will insist, they are "cutting back". Unless one happens to be a proffesional arborist clearing limbs from power lines, "pruning" is only something one does when one's prescription runs out.

This sort of interaction can be demoralizing, and is thus best avoided all together. The next time you feel compelled to explain or defend your craft to others—don't. Just lock yourself in the shed and sharpen all your tools. Oil them, too. Mutter to yourself if it helps. There's nothing crazy about that

But sooner or later, you'll have to step foot outside—probably to limb-up that *Stewartia* you've been thinking about—and as soon as you do, you will be relegated, once more, to the gardener's asylum. There, you will join all us other other freak pruners, compulsive seed-collectors, blathering composters, nut-job mulchers and crackpot propagators which polite society prefers to keep at a distance. We're a ragtag bunch to be sure, but at least around here the hydrangeas always bloom.

Reason #8

<u>Two Days, Max</u>

Imagine waking up, one fine Spring morn, and as you stand before your dresser, naked, telling yourself that this is the year—*this*—at long last, will be the year you keep track of all your daily fashion choices. That's right, every outfit, every accessory, every pair of shoes, every brand, every day. You'll go out this very morning and buy yourself a little notebook, a nice one, to be your official fashion journal.

Yes, it's settled—a Fashion Journal. In fact, go ahead and put that on the cover. Use capital letters, or a fancy font. Each morning, after you dress yourself, you'll make an entry in this *FASHION JOURNAL* describing your selections and your reasons for those particular choices.

For example: *Tuesday the 13th. Rain expected—*

rubber boots and a hat, ho hum. Any wardrobe changes made during the day will be duly noted and explained. *Friday evening: going to a show—sequins, boa, hip-waders and a monocle. That opera won't know what hit it!* And any resulting successes or failures will be honestly addressed for future reference. *Friday evening P.S.: no longer allowed at the opera.*

You've had this idea before. Seemingly every year you promise a faithful and diligent fashion telling. It just makes sense, after all. What better way to improve your comfort, style and budget than to keep strict record of every decision? Though such meticulous bookkeeping may seem daunting, the rewards are numerous. This year, you will have a quick reference for coworkers who want the source of those *divine* macrame suspenders you sported last week. This time around, when tempted by that tie-die silk kimono that always seems to taunt you from the shelves in Autumn, you can flip to your notes from last year and see the underlined warning: *NOT WORTH $2500!* See now, *that's* why you couldn't make rent, got evicted, and moved in with your sister last year.

Or, say your gut tells you that it's probably okay to

wear a latex body suit 3 days in a row (in which case it might be time for a gut check, but that's another matter entirely). Let's see how that went over in March. *Bad idea. One day was fun, two days quirky, third day got fired.* Well there you have it—two days, max for a latex body suit.

This *FASHION JOURNAL* will be fantastic, it will be fabulous, as anything to do with fashion by all rights ought to be. It will finally take the guesswork out of dressing yourself. I don't know about you, but for me, getting dressed tends to involve a lot of guesswork. What's clean, which ragged pants can still dodge decency laws etc.— but you! If you can only stay committed to your *FASHION JOURNAL*, you will effortlessly repeat past successes and avoid prior mistakes. When was that fabulous sale at Urban, uh, Republic ... and Beyond ... er, Mama Bahamas—whatever, this is not my strong suit—when was it? *April 26th -29th.* How many pairs of gauntlets did you need for the work week, without having to do laundry? *Six pairs of gauntlets: one a day and one just in case.* I don't know why you'd need a backup pair of gauntlets, but hey, it's your journal. And what was the name of that street vendor who sold you a dozen handmade Looney Tunes belt buckles for 20 bucks? *Pomegranate Thompson—but the*

Foghorn Leghorn buckle looked a lot like the Daffy Duck.
Even so, that last one was the deal of the decade, if you ask
me.

It will be difficult, tedious at times, but if this is
indeed to be the year of the *FASHION JOURNAL*, and you
are able to stick with your daily entries to the end, you will
have achieved something no gardener ever has. For every
year, gardeners fill the idle moments of the off-season with
similar ambitions of record-keeping. Not with respect to
fashion, thank god (oh, what a tedium of vests!), but rather a
GARDEN JOURNAL. I, myself, have no fewer than five
such titled notebooks buried in shame around the office. In
each, the entries begin orderly and regularly, peppered with
careful wit and orderly little sketches; maybe a short poem
here and there. These last through about January, all the
while decaying into unrelated (yet still bulleted, for some
reason) lists, margin scribbles, and unfinished thoughts. By
the time February rolls around, if the pages aren't just blank,
they contain only a smattering of plant names, barely legible
and truncated from all context or syntax. Here we go, here's a
good one: *Feb. 2011. Ham. 'Diane'.*

Ah yes, 2011. What a year.

After February, several months slip by un-journaled, tumbling forever into the chasm of gardens past. Whoever shall know what became of a garden during these empty weeks?

Then, from out of nowhere, perhaps spurred by the frenzied assault of May, one last entry emerges to stand foolish and tall against the gathering forces of chaos. A volley of year-to-date estimations, plants planted, transplants transplanted, and seeds sown. The weather, germination, the thinning and damping off. Mulchings and Weedings. A page or two of not-to-scale sketches and best-guess Latin, hollering for order with a final gasp.

Then silence once more, into obscurity and the black hole that is the remaining year. Left behind: the smell of smeared ink, the reek of desperation, and the ellipses of failure …

As a gardener, these half-baked annals of gardening activity are to be your legacy. Posterity will look back at your gibberish and question the sanity of its forbears. Your well-titled *GARDEN* JOURNALs will provide, not the timeless wisdom and memory of halcyon rose beds and harvest moons, but rather the unsentimental clutter of attics and storage units, saved by anonymous descendents only to assuage the guilt of not understanding the feeble madness of their ancestors. They will heap your sorry tomes in boxes rather than garbage bins only because, by their very quantity, if not quality, they must have meant something, to someone, once.

As for me, I can only hope my children's children might one day stumble onto some inky scribble of haunting prescience penned in the margin of one of my crumbling journals. For this will be my message, my immortality and my estate:

Feb. 19, 2012: Sarc. ~~*ruse*~~/*<u>confusa</u>? (no berries)x3 gal.s Nwcorner. Too big?*

No berries, indeed. Words to live by. You won't find that in any *FASHION JOURNAL.*

Reason #9

<u>The Service Was Terrible</u>

Let's just start by saying that rain would never make it in the service industry. Precipitation, I mean. That fickle and flighty dripline in the sky. From the gardener's (admittedly biased) perspective, rain does not excel at its given vocation.

Think about it: rain is like that one server at the restaurant with meticulously bad timing. You know the sort— lunges in repeatedly while you attempt to decipher chapters of pun-riddled entrees; lobs small talk into your efforts like cheerful grenades; hides in the back for forty minutes when your glass or breadbasket is empty; cracks pepper over anything in sight; leaves abruptly and then swoops in ten seconds later, all grins and good-intentions, asking how your food is, how EVERYTHING IS! right after you've stuffed half a cheeseburger into your face.

Unfortunately, in the zero-star restaurant of gardening, this particular server, Rain, is your only option. He's got tenure or something. His dad must own the place. If you want to eat out, say, to take the week off from hoses and sprinklers, odds are you'll be stuck at his table. He is the sole provider of an important and valuable service which one can't help but speculate might be improved by a bit of customer feedback. I mean, besides those comment cards they leave with the bill. I don't imagine he reads those. And even if he did—

—Oh, shoot, look, I know you just sat down to read this, but I think he must have seen you ... Rain, you know, the server I was telling you about? He's heading your way now. *Shh!* Look, pretend you have no interest in gardening. Don't acknowledge him, don't—oh, for crying out—

"—Hi there folks, my name is Rain! Looks like I'll be taking care of you this year. How are we all doing tonight? You feel that Spring breeze in the air? Well I bet you're hungry to get going outside. First things first, I noticed your fruit trees are about to bloom, so I'll just leave enough cold drizzle to get a bit of blossom wilt going. There we go, that should take care of your cherries, anyway. Who needs cherries, right? Okay, now, since it is springtime and I know you have a lot to catch up on, I'll make myself scarce for a few days during the work week—my associate Gorgeous Balmy Sunshine here will take care of you while you're stuck at the office—but don't worry, I'll be back just as soon as you get off work on Friday. That's right, since you folks are such great customers, your old pal Rain is going to stick around all weekend. And as long as that schedule works for you, we'll just keep it up for the next two or three months."

By which point, you will have fallen hopelessly behind for the rest of the year.

Now, I know normal people, too, must deal with the vagaries of weather, not just gardeners. But whereas most folks turn a wary eye to the forecast a few times a year when vacations or barbecues loom on the horizon, gardeners spend all year stuck at the table with this same bad waiter and his— oh, god, he's coming back. Hurry, run to the bathroom or—

"—Hi again, folks! I just heard a rumor that you took a few days off to work on a hardscaping project. Is that true? Well, that's a special occasion! I want you to know I'll be right here for you the whole time. If there's anything you need, just let me know. I've got everything from sprinkles to monsoon. Ooh, and I can't recommend the special highly enough: this week only, we've got a freak hailstorm that would just pair perfectly with that concrete work you're trying to do. No? Well, how about some spotty showers? They're fantastic, they let up just long enough for you to get all set up and then come dripping back right when you're about to start your project. Fantastic, we'll go with that."

Every time, I swear.

But it's not just the fact that you're looking at an outdoor hobby and so must expose yourself to the elements in order to recreate, plenty of other saps are in the same boat (including, I suppose, boaters themselves). The gardener can run back inside with his tail between his legs or just throw on some rain gear as easily as any kite-flier, mountain biker or extreme, outdoor *knitteur* would. The *garden*, on the other hand, is not nearly so mobile. Your vegetable bed cannot storm out of the restaurant in a huff. The health and well-being of your plants, and thus your *own* health and well-being (if, like most gardeners, your sense of empathy aligns uselessly with the vegetative world) are hugely impacted by the service of Rain and its—*argh*, speak of the devil, here he comes again. Look, pretend we're in a very intense, private conversation and maybe he'll go away—

"— *Heyyy* again, guys! Just realized, I forgot to discuss Summer with you. Now, unfortunately I'm not going to be available a lot of the time. I see here you're leaving to go on vacation for a week right when your garden is the most thirsty. Looks like I'll be gone then. Whew! Getting hot out here, huh? Hmm … now, I will try to stop by for your garden party; no garden party is complete without thunderstorms! And I'll be sure to swing by for a solid couple days in late Summer to see how your tomatoes are ripening. Seems like a lot of them end up splitting, is that normal? But that's about it for Summer, I'll leave a couple extra orders of Drought to tide you over for the season; it comes with powdery mildew for all your late season perennials, squashes, that sort of thing, and—of course— a huge water bill that I just know you're going to love! Thanks, folks, you've been great. Feel free to fill out one of those comment cards with your bill and be sure to come back soon. Thanks again, take care!"

See what I mean about the service? Oh well, at least he's gone for a while. Whatever you do, don't leave a tip, it only encourages him—oh, lord, what now? He's coming back. No, no, no, why on Earth is he sitting down!?

"Wow! Are you folks still here? No one ever sticks around this long! I hope you don't mind if I pull up a chair. I think it's the Autumn air, it just makes me want to park it for a while. <*Yawn!*> Oh, man, I am spent! Might be a few, five, six months before I can get up again. Well, as long as we're sharing a table … have I ever shown you my collection of storms? Here, I'll just line them up one after another so you can enjoy—wait, you guys were done gardening for the year, right?"

I guess we are, now.

Why do I keep coming here?

Reason #10

The Red-Handled Devils

Or, as you may know them better ... Felcos.

I know, I know, you're thinking, *now wait just a cotton-pickin' minute*, (your inner monologue is peppered with old-timey slang, don't deny it), *what's wrong with Felcos? How could everyone's favorite brand of high-end Swiss pruners present any sort of reason not to garden, much less command such a sinister title? Sure, they're a bit pricey, but what quality tool isn't?*

Your protest is duly noted, and duly rejected.

The problem, as I see it, is that the use of this— admittedly superb—pruning device (*Author's note: Despite indications to the contrary, at the time of this writing, the author has not received any promotional consideration from*

Felco. The author is, however, open to promotional consideration. From Felco, or anyone else. The author thinks, at the time of this writing, it's about time he got a sweet endorsement deal. Maybe the author will go talk to Corona if he doesn't hear from Felco. The author's French is not great, anyway, he realizes, and his German is even worse. At the time of this writing, the author wonders what language they speak over at Corona) can, by itself, instigate a sort of snowballing existential crisis, the likes of which will almost certainly leave you wishing you'd never wrapped your greedy little fingers around those sexy red handles, and will just as certainly have you cursing this whole gardening thing as bad for the soul. (Gardening, as it turns out, is full of snowballing existential crises. Just you wait.)

You see, the first time you feel the smooth grip of those Felcos melt into your hand, becoming one with it in a way no tool ever has; the first time you squeeze and it is the squeeze of man and machine at long last united, of blade forged to very flesh and articulated for a common purpose— that first effortless *<snick>* of finely honed blade slicing through a branch like butter, and you will experience what I speak of. There, in your garden, as you innocuously perform

a more-or-less mundane task, you will have achieved a peak life experience—*BAM!* Just like that. Out in the backyard, wearing your grubby gardening clothes, maybe high up on a ladder, or with your head stuck in a *Rhododendron*—wherever it may be, you will have realized the great joy of an action perfected. Then, blindsided by the unexpected, inappropriate inertia of that joy, you will fall to your knees and weep. You will have been … caught *Red-Handled.*
(Additional author's note: Come on, Felco, Corona, anyone —"Caught Red-Handled"? That's a great slogan. I'm giving you gold, here. The least you could do is comp me some free pruners. At the time of this writing, the author has still not received one damn bit of promotional consideration.)

I'm quite convinced this happens all the time. If it all sounds a bit cheesy but otherwise harmless, just wait for the next part.

That would be the part where you realize that you are on your knees weeping over the (admittedly inspiring) performance of a simple pair of pruners—and the shame *clobbers* you. For what does this say about you? About your life? That you are so moved by something so incidental, so minute and trivial? You, who perhaps did not weep at the birth of your own child. You, who gawks at televised disasters and tragedies with naught but a *tsk* and a shake of the head. What can this possibly mean if your emotional gauge is so miscalibrated that some arbitrary winter pruning has you red-lined and sobbing at the unexpected beauty of it all, while much more deserving events—say, I don't know, your daughter going off to college or the movie *Bambie*—slip by without so much as a sniffle? What can it mean that, as the maelstrom of modern life tumbles you headlong past landmark occasions and scrapbook memories, you have arrived at the eye of the storm, and this, *this*, is suddenly your moment to savor it all, to finally appreciate and find meaning in the otherwise swirling chaos?

It means one (or both) of two things. One: you are a sociopath. You genuinely have no emotional connection to the world of people and their problems; your Felco-induced rapture was nothing more than errant hormones and crossed wires. Or, two: you have become so hardened to the world, have so fortified the front lines of everyday emotional attack and erected such massive bulwarks against life's siege of Halmark moments, that you could not help but overlook some small, unimportant flaw in your armor. In this case, finely-machined pruners just happen to be the exposed exhaust port of your death star.

Neither is a condition to which one normally aspires, and quite frankly it sounds like some sort of therapy is in order either way.

The third option, I suppose, is that you have simply become a gardener. It's still not a great face to see in the mirror (and don't think you're getting out of therapy that easily), but at least you're in good company. Your support group meets every day down at the garden center.

Of course, you could have avoided all of this if you'd simply steered clear of the rocky shores of gardening, over whose crashing surf trills the piercing call of the alluring, red-handled sirens. For no one can resist their song.

Really, those things ought to come with a warning.

Reason #11

<u>Zero Chance Of Iced Teastorms</u>

So it's hot out. Well, at least 90°F—is that hot for you? We'll say it's whatever passes for hot where you come from. In the Pacific Northwest, anything over 75 is considered hot. (And anything under 70 is cold; we don't do extremes here.) In any case, it's way too hot out. You just spent eight or more hours on your feet, out in the aforementioned hotness, veiled in a half-inch slathering of SPF 300. Working. Maybe your job involves lifting and moving hundreds of plants while doling out sweat-stained shreds of customer service to red-faced patrons—maybe not. But probably, in this case, it does.

You are dehydrated, on the verge of heat stroke. Maybe you start to hear voices.

Find a new job! they might say. *You've made unwise career choices!*

But then, just when you can take no more—salvation. It's quitting time. That's right, you're free!

You tear off clothes even as you stagger to your car— which, if 90° is too hot, then the inside of your car is, by this point, a fully-functioning kiln. This is a perfect opportunity to bake any unfired pottery you have lying around. Once on the road, you suffer hallucinations the whole traffic-snarled, asphalt-melting commute home.

Your visions are of snowstorms and iced tea—iced teastorms. Sometime later, and no time later (for time has ceased to exist; it melted, Dali-esque, somewhere on the freeway on-ramp), you arrive home. You stagger through the door, half-naked and delirious. Now, at long last, you may assert some measure of control over your own (dis)comfort. You get to choose how to unwind, how to cool off, how to relax.

So what do you do?

The sane person has any number of perfectly reasonable options. Take a cold shower; draw the blinds and turn off the lights; watch TV; find the sweet spot between three oscillating fans; stick your head in the freezer. Even for those courageous—or masochistic—enough to return outside, there are numerous refreshments available: go jump in a lake; sit in the shade with a keg of iced tea (someone's gotta make that iced teastorm dream a reality); follow the creepy, warped siren-call of your local ice cream truck and rediscover popsicles; skulk to a big-box store and splurge on an AC unit you'll use two weeks out of the year; stop by the kids-only wading pool at the city park and act like a proud parent; linger in the cool rush of air conditioned store fronts.

All great choices. But since no gardener has ever been mistaken for a sane person, I have this nagging suspicion you do something else, don't you? Because the garden does not take days off, after all, and, after all, that lilac stump you cut down weeks ago isn't going to just dig itself out.

Brilliant! Yes, that's what you, in your fevered idiocy, decide to do—*remove a stump.* In the most merciless, sun-broiled corner of the yard, at the hottest time of day you lug out the pick and mattock and **REMOVE A STUMP**. I don't quite know which combination of font size/emphasis best conveys the absurdity of this decision, but rest assured

hyperbole is not a concern. ***YOU REMOVE A STUMP!!!***
Congratulations on whatever heat-induced malady you incur
to go along with that lovely blister-red you'll be sporting on
every patch of exposed skin— you deserve it.

As a gardener, you will reliably and consistently
direct your attention to such appalling tasks as this
throughout the year, no matter how garishly contraindicated
by thermometer, barometer, or common sense. For the sport
of gardening is extreme, and not at all subject to sissy
weather delays. You just slam back a Lime Blast
Gardenade® and get out there. Before you know it, you will
be tap dancing atop ladders in a gale. You will carve
irrigation trenches during a biblical deluge. You will conduct
thunderstorms from the heavens with extendable pole
pruners. You will stand motionless in the cold, excising bits
of deadwood from shrubs while frostbite settles in,
necrotizing your limbs and rendering *you* the one in need of
some pruning. In a crucible of lunacy, you will proclaim *this
very moment* to be the only one suitable for planting 400 tulip
bulbs, damn the tornado warning. You will squint to see the
myopic wisdom of transplanting and dividing after heavy
rain when the soil consists of sloppy potters' clay (this,

perhaps, the source of all that unfired pottery you've been car-baking during the Summer commute), which medium sticks to and coats and weighs down every tool, article of clothing, high spirit or exposed bit of anatomy in play.

You will, as previously mentioned, find it somehow advisable to attack stumps in the roaring heat of hell.

Why all this madness? It's not as though you are deprived of meteorological data. You *see* the weather report; you hear the words coming out of the meteorologist's mouth. You may even consult the minute-by-minute forecast on your phone. But precisely *none* of the information thus acquired is ever able to navigate your sensorium and twisted logic to actually *inform* your actions. The state of the weather is either completely irrelevant to, or cryptically justifies the timing of the task at hand.

It's like talking to a stalk of corn. Any scrap of good sense and rationale will quickly rot in that tumbling compost bin the gardener mistakes for a brain, all dignity and wisdom gobbled up as fertilizer for the platonic garden-to-be. And that is why you will never just stay inside, never taste the cold sweet kiss of a popsicle and never dance in the refreshing drizzle of an after-work iced teastorm. Your extended forecast is, by your own making, a bleak one.

Reason #12

<u>The Green Reaper</u>

Sit down, would-be gardener, if you dare, and hear the tale of the Green Reaper.

Know that all who turn the earth to sow their seeds do beg his ghoulish visitation in the night. All who pray for rain upon their crop will only be parched by his flaming scythe. All who dig will mark graves; all who plant will weep.

Those who have laid eyes upon his—

"Oh, hey, guys! What's going on here? A story?"

...

Those who have laid eyes upon—

"Because I love stories. Almost as much as I love plants. Too bad I can't seem to keep them alive, heh-heh. But, you know, what are you gonna do? The Green Reaper can't very well have a green thumb, now, can I?"

…

Those who have laid eyes upon his horrible visage have gone mad. They say his bones are made of rotted wood —

"Whoa, no way! Is this a story about me? The Green Reaper? Because I'm totally the Green Reaper!"

…

They say his bones are made of rotted wood, his long hair a tangle of blackened roots, reeking of decay. Under his tattered vest—

"Yeah! The wood bones, the hair, the vest; that's totally me! Check it out! What's the matter, you don't believe me? Here, let me see that little Japanese Maple you just planted … mhmm … and … voila! Verticillium wilt!"

…

His targets are arbitrary. He strikes with cruelty and feels no remorse—

"Hey, come on now! I wouldn't say *no* remorse. I mean, I can't feel too bad about it—this is the one thing I'm good at, after all. It's what I do. I wouldn't expect *you* to show crippling remorse about … narrating stories … or whatever it is you do. But still, y'know, I'm not blind. I'm sure that little maple must have cost a pretty penny."

—no remorse. His destruction spares neither the prized, nor the sentimental. With a sweep of the arm he claims beauty, vitality, and the little Japanese Maple one carefully and tearfully dug from one's deceased grandmother's garden to save it from developers who were bulldozing the lot.

" … Oh, dang. Really? Wait, is that actually in the story? Huh. Well, now I feel a bit bad. That's sweet, though. From your grandma's place, huh? Were you able to save anything else? What about this cool-looking dwarf conifer here—ohhhhh. Shoot. Was that … ? Man, I gotta learn to be less hands-on."

Everything he touches turns brown and crumbles to dust. The merest idle gesture brings death and despair for the irreplaceably rare dwarf conifer one's father brought back from his travels in Northern China.

"Yikes! I. Am. Sorry. There, I said it. Jeez. I'm sorry I killed your … what was that? A spruce? No, wait *this* one over here, *this* is a—was—a spruce. Okay, I'm sorry for that one, too. That was my bad."

His manner is clumsy and brutish. He strikes with all the grace of a drunkard, spreading aphid, mite, and scale with every wicked, spastic touch. One's favorite, ancient spruce is lousy in seconds. If ever you see the wretched clod stumbling toward your garden, run! Run with all the—

"—Drunkard? Look, I'll have you know I had one glass of red wine before this. I was *on my way home from dinner* when I overheard your little story here and stopped by. You know what that's called? Being neighborly. You ought to try it sometime. And you know what? I don't think I particularly like your story. You certainly didn't win me over with the 'horrible visage' bit at the beginning. You think I asked to look like this? Come on, buddy, I'm just trying to do my job and it's not my fault—*whoop!* Aaaaah!"

…

"I—I'm alright. I'm … Okay. Jeez. Why was there a hose here right in the—oh boy. That wasn't your perennial bed I just fell into, was it? Yeesh. Okay, but some of those were already dead, right?"

…

A broad swath of unfathomable devastation rains in

his wake. Ruin is his name. Dickish recklessness his calling card. A single moronic fall and he scatters pestilence upon delicate woodland perennials and ancient, stalwart peonies alike. One wonders, in one's misery, just what one did to deserve his company.

"What you did? Well, for starters, I mean, you planted a garden. What did you think would happen? You're the one narrating the story of the Green Reaper. Did you think you were somehow exempt? You spend time and money growing plants, and I kill them. It's simple. That's the deal. That's how it works and you should know—oh, my god … are those ripe plums on that tree? Dude, plums are my *faaavorite,* you have no idea."

He is unstoppable. Voracious. Insatiable. He will not be turned away until every blossom wilts, every leaf curls, every fruit rots.

"Take it easy, Mr. Drama Queen. I'm not going to kill your fruit tree. I just want one of those plums. Let's see … now I'm pretty sure, if I put a glove on my hand, I can pick one without hurting the tree. I think that's how it works, anyway. Man, it's been a long time since reaper school. Aaand … there we go, just like I—ahhh … crap. Okay, that's

90

not how it works. My bad. You might be able to just prune off that limb and save the rest of the … well, maybe not. Nope, that's definitely the whole tree. Man, I didn't even know I could do bacterial canker. Wow. Come on now, you've got to be at least a *little* bit impressed; that was fast, right? Mmm, oh well, sorry about that. Good plum, though, anyone want a bite?

The ravaged gardener howls: be gone, cursed creature! Return to the compost heap whence you came! Nevermore shall I till the earth. Nevermore shall I tend the crops. Evermore shall I … switch to model airplanes, or something. Anything but this!

"You want me to leave, is that it? No one wants me around? I get it. All right, fine, you asked for it. I'll leave. Right after I—*nananana*! Ha! Ha! Your hedge! What? That'll teach you to incur my wrath. Damn straight, I've got wrath. Mom said I'm not wrathful enough. HOW'S THAT, MOM!? I just took out this guys laurel hedge!"

The Green Reaper at long last takes his leave—a bitter, sorry soul. Childhood issues rear their head with every miserable step. His only recourse is pettiness; he lashes out blindly with blight and drought and mysterious fungus, mistakenly claiming one's neighbor's laurel hedge.

"Neighbor? Meh, whatever, that guy was probably on my list anyway. I'm outta here, suckers! I've got a few thousand Daphne to kill for no reason!"

…

No garden is safe; no gardener spared. Beware, beware and then beware some more! Beware the Green Reaper. Seriously, though. Beware. That guy's an ass.

"I heard that!"

I don't care!

Reason #13
Bread Season

If you think about it, modern grocery stores are amazing—a wonder of the modern world. They really ought to be considered one of the crown jewels of all human achievement, if you ask me.

Which no one did, but as the majority of this book was neither asked for nor, by and large, warranted, I'm not about to stop now. Furthermore, if you're still with me, and still considering gardening as anything but a startlingly communicable disease for which the world's best minds ought, by all rights, be developing some sort of a vaccine, then something tells me you're sticking it out to the end as well.

Where was I?

Ah yes—grocery stores, for some reason. Those 24/7,

coin-operated cornucopiae, which spill out into baskets, parking lots, and trunks every conceivable product to sate the material needs of our civilization. From kiwi fruit to cotton swabs; from AAA batteries to chorizo; indeed from diet cherry cola to microwaveable burritos—all the bare necessities our ancestors risked life and limb to glean from whatever harsh natural environment they had the misfortune of inhabiting—we are now able to sweep into our shopping cart without a thought but for the timeless dilemma of which ice-cream flavor among nine dozen will come closest to completing us on a given evening. (The answer is always the same: spumoni.)

Now perhaps, in the checkout line, the thought might occur to you (pensive reader and shopper that you are) that you have, in the act of grocery shopping, severed the age-old link between production and consumption. For you have come down squarely on the side of the consumer, lodging yourself there as though fallen from great heights into a sucking tide flat. While you yourself may assemble the purchased ingredients into picnic lunches and soft-tacos and tom-collinses, you feel you must admit that you stepped in fairly late along the supply chain. Unless—I don't know, unless you grind your own chorizo at home. You don't, do you?

Let's say, for the sake of argument, you *don't* grind your own chorizo at home. How else might you go about re-inserting your own cog into the great, shrieking Rube-Goldberg contraption of food production?

My personal favorite (and ultimately meaningless) middle finger to the convenience of grocery stores is to walk right past the spray-bottles and tubs of whipped cream to the shelf containing actual heavy cream, in little cartons. These I purchase with a keen but misplaced smugness and a thumb to my nose: *nananana* you robber-barons of—hmm, well, again, I'm not sure who exactly gets the finger in this scenario. Someone ought to feel my scorn. In any case, I take the cream home, pour it into a bowl and then spend the better part of a half-hour attempting to whip it into a light, fluffy submission. After a few rounds with the whisk, however, I'm inevitably forced to tap out at the mercy of crippling hand and arm cramps. The epic battle leaves me with nothing but a slightly thickened, still quite liquid—we'll call it "agitated"—cream to pour unappatizingly over my cobbler, pudding or what have you. Oh, the satisfaction.

You can see why the better-traveled route to ownership of ones edibles comes in the form of that erstwhile topic-at-large: gardening. Standing there, in the checkout line, you're thinking: why don't I just grown my own damn kiwis?

And you may, you may indeed grow your own damn kiwis. But of course, it won't stop there; it never does. Soon you'll be sowing gherkins and runner beans and Danver half-longs and patty-pans and all sorts of things with ridiculous names you'd never before pin as foodstuffs. You'll be tilling the lawn under and swapping your boxwood for blueberries. You'll give kohlrabi a shot, why not? You'll flaunt the wealth of your harvest with a hail of zucchinis like dollar bills at a strip-club. You'll make it rain. And herein can be found true satisfaction. For the fruits of your labor will be (relatively) cheap, plentiful, and delicious.

On the surface, that may seem like a good thing.

But sooner or later, the dark side of agricultural prosperity will creep like a shadow across your many trellises. Because the more success you enjoy—the more bountiful your harvest, the tastier your crop—the more intolerably bland grocery store produce will start to seem.

Mealy apples, flavorless carrots, brand name strawberries all pith and no soul, insipid, injection-molded tomatoes, all slathered with the same repulsive wax. Whatever convenience is to be gained in the year-round availability of such worldly crops at the local market is soon lost when the godawful mush is spit out into the kitchen sink in a nauseous quarrel between disgust and disdain. Now, whenever your own, vastly superior, backyard produce section lies dormant in the offseason, you simply won't be able to stomach the thought of all that neatly stacked, sprayed, and color-coded fruit-and-vegetable-substitute proffered at $3.99 per pound one aisle over from the diapers and paper towels.

It really is quite difficult to express the profundity of this difference between home-grown and store-bought produce. It is akin to describing the subjective experience of a fantastic drug to someone who tried tiramisu, once, and found that the rum-soaked ladyfingers made their head spin. It is like trying to convey the crippling emotional state wrought by that dream you had about the mailman and the zoo and the baby. (It was just ... devastating.) To those who have never experienced it firsthand, a sun-warmed, fresh-from-the-vine cherry tomato is to a rank-and-file Roma what

Breeple is to the color Blue. *Breeple* being, of course, a pretty fantastic color you didn't know existed until just now.

It may be more helpful to consider what would happen if you were afforded the opportunity to grow any other grocery store department's offerings, from seed, in your raised beds out back. (Then it again, it may not be, but since it's bound to be at least a little bit entertaining, why don't we just see where I'm heading with this?) So let's consider, shall we, a different kind of harvest.

What if, for example, baked goods grew from seed? What if, there, next to the spinning sunglasses rack at your local hardware store/garden center, was a whole rack of organic bakery seeds? Or maybe you get a seed catalog in the mail—hot loaves for the upcoming year steaming seductively on the cover. Either way, the choices are endless: French croissants; heirloom muffins; mixed donut blends; hearty homestyle loaves like your dad made (is that a hint of molasses?); buttery dinner rolls; obscure eastern European pastries you can't pronounce so you know they're good; the finest English crumpets; sandwich breads; bread for toast; crusty loaves for dipping into soup; rye; flatbreads; cranberry orange scones; crostini; breadsticks; sourdough; baguettes galore—even croutons if you so desire—all lined up neatly in tidy little sachets. A couple bucks a pack *et voila*! you've got crullers to last you the year. Come September you're giving them away by the dozen to any neighbor who'll take them.

Unfortunately, as with any harvest, bread season only lasts so long, and with the first Autumn rains, the sliced bread peels from its crust, the maple bars go to seed, and the naan begins to rot. After several months enjoying the fruits of your own world-class carb-garden, you now must confront the reality of the grocery store bakery once more.

As you hang your head and skulk down the aisles upon which you once relied for all your leavened needs, you now find the selection wanting, to say the least. Where once you seem to remember shopping an assortment of tolerable, if predictable, pre-packaged baked goods, you are now shocked to find only a single bag of past pull-date, off brand English muffins and two kinds of stale hot dog buns. Oh wait —there's also a loaf of unlabeled wheat bread, which appears to have been previously opened … yes, there's definitely about a third of the loaf missing. So I guess that's a previously owned loaf of wheat bread?

Good lord, you think, how do people live like this?

Why doesn't everyone grow their own bread?

There now—wasn't that a fun, helpful illustration?

You see, such will be the incredible letdown of the produce aisle once you have embarked upon your ill-fated gardening journey. The modern mega-grocer will become, ever-so-slightly, less awesome. And do you really want to live in a world where the modern grocery store is anything less than a crown jewel of human achievement? Save yourself, I implore you. Be content with "fruits" and "vegetables" without resorting to quotation marks. Do not subject yourself to the cognitive dissonance reverberating between the fresh fruit of a tomato vine and the so-called "tomatoes" piled high betwixt pyramids of yams and pomegranates at Grubmart. Are the store-bought versions great? No, but you don't have to know that. And you certainly don't need to know what a Danver half-long is.

If you desperately need to maintain the illusion of control over your personal food chain, just do what I do: buy a carton of cream (aisle nine, I believe), pour it into a bowl, and take out some aggression. There's nothing like fresh, hassled cream poured over hot apple pie to kindle the warm glow of satisfaction.

Reason #14

<u>Triage</u>

Yes, hello! Please! Can I have your attention? Quiet down, everyone!

<Airhorn blast>

That's better, thank you.

Welcome to Gardener's Hospital triage unit. As it happens, I'm the only garden doctor on call today, so you hopeless lot are stuck with me. Now, if you'll all calm down and shut up about this year's Great Plant Picks for one second, we can get to your injuries. Whoa! Please! Please, one at a time! And if you'll be so good as to remove your sun hats, there are quite a few of you to process and we are full to the *brim* in here. Heh-heh. No, wait, the place is *brimming* with injured gardeners. Heh-heh—sorry, sorry—okay, who's first up?

You there, with the swollen face. Bee stings? Let me guess, you knew there was a nest in the ground, but figured they wouldn't bother you if you didn't bother them? No? Am I close? Oh, wait, I've got it: you discovered a yellow-jacket nest in your prized species *Rhododendron,* and with the garden tour coming up on Saturday you had no choice but to try to remove it yourself? Take one for the tour, did you? Bingo. Okay, move to that far corner if you would. No—I swear, it doesn't look that bad. I'm sure the hideous swelling will go down by Saturday.

And you—holding the back of your head and limping —I'd know that combo anywhere; you stood up directly underneath that damn birdhouse for the umpteenth time. Then, in a fit of rage, you drop-kicked the thing into your neighbor's yard to be rid of it once and for all, most likely breaking your toe in the process … Ha, I knew it! That corner please. Birdhouses are no joke, people; they will ruin you.

Aaand, let's see now … I'm noticing several folks with their hair sticking up and faces twitching, you lot clearly discovered long-forgotten buried electrical wires while digging, we'll put you over here. If you could please divide yourselves into two groups, one for low-voltage incidents and one for high-voltage, it would make our job a lot easier. He-he, you all look like you had too much coffee. Sorry, sorry—unprofessional.

Oh—Okay, I should have asked this right off the bat: to everyone who slipped while aggressively sawing a branch at an inadvisable angle, has anyone failed to stop the bleeding on their own? No? Okay, good job, people, that buys us some time. All of you can take a seat over there and carry on wincing. Just to be sure, you do understand—conceptually, anyway—the properties of a saw which allow it to cut through wood? And you further grasp that these properties do not disappear when the saw is not in contact with wood? Right, so there's no reason to assume your own flesh and bone should bear some sort of mystical immunity to the saw's nominal task? Right, just checking. Remember to keep that pressure firm!

You there, with the serene expression on your face, what's wrong with you? Please, speak up! ... No, I'm sorry, your mouth is moving but there's just no sound coming out—ohhh, wait a minute, I know what's going on here. Are there any more of you? Okay, this is actually a fairly common ailment. For anyone rendered speechless by the fleeting, singular beauty of a spring-blooming ephemeral: rest assured, your muteness should be temporary. Like, six out of ten times, at least. To more quickly reverse the awestruck condition, feel free to browse this photo collection of horsetails invading gardens ... That's it, just look at those bastards—whoa-ho! There we go, good as new! Cursing like gardeners once again.

And let's see ... back injuries. All of you stooped over, lying flat or trying to yoga a disc into place: frankly, I don't even know what you're doing here. As gardeners you should already have a chiropractor or a massage therapist on retainer. If you cannot afford these services, then either learn to pace yourselves or consider jigsaw puzzles as a safer alternative hobby. Let's not clog up the ER with what, for folks of your lifestyle, amounts to a paper cut. You don't see computer programmers crowding into the ER complaining of eye strain. Ice and ibuprofen ... repeat.

Oh boy, here we go, this one's a doozy—ladders! Please listen up! If you were involved in a ladder incident, we'll have to redirect you to the parking lot, where we have a separate triage tent set up. I'm sorry, there are just too many of you to process here. I don't know what it is with you people; I swear you'd fall and break something just looking at a ladder. Four out of five garden doctors agree: stay away from ladders, why not! That's right ... single file, please. Help yourself to a pair of crutches on your way out.

Okay, thank you for your patience everyone, this will go a lot faster with those ladder cases gone. Unfortunately, I have to confess, there is no triage tent in the parking lot. I feel a little bad about that. But, in my defense, it wouldn't do any good if there were. We'd fix them up and then as soon as the casts came off, they'd be lunging with extendable pole-pruners from the top of 15-foot orchard ladders that same afternoon. What!? Don't look at me like that, you know it's true.

Now, if you're all done passing judgment ... I promise we'll get to everyone. While you are waiting to be seen, nurses will be circulating with tetanus boosters. Is there anyone who doesn't need a tetanus booster? Ha Ha! Sorry, bad joke, of course everyone needs one! In fact, take two! Lockjaw and gardeners go together like racquetball and bruises ... what, no one here has ever played racquetball?

Forget it, trust me, it's an appropriate simile.

Okay, who's up next? Heat stroke? Honestly, folks, It's 95° out there! What was so important you all had to be out in the garden, anyway? … Mhmm. Let me get this straight, all— *six, seven, eight*—nine of you had old stumps that needed removing? In the middle of a heat wave? Couldn't wait? Yes, I see the urgency. We wouldn't want those stumps drying out, would we? *I get called in on a Saturday for this*—well, I'm sorry to say you'll all be placed in air-conditioned isolation rooms looking out on your respective gardens until such a time as you can sit for five minutes sipping lemonade without lunging for a pick-and-mattock. Trust me, it's for your own good.

Let's see, what else … those of you who decided to tackle a huge tree-removal or pruning job because you were too cheap to pay for an arborist, and against the repeated warnings of a spouse, please line up in order of how many bones you need set and how many warnings you ignored. Next time listen to your partner. Here is a pamphlet on swallowing your pride, with a list of certified arborists in the back. Anyone reckless enough to use a chainsaw in the process, please forfeit said instrument of chaos and dismemberment to local gardening authorities; your privileges have been revoked.

In fact, why doesn't everyone in the room here just turn in their chainsaws now. Come on, let's have them. If you're not here because of one, it's only a matter of time before you are. Sir, I can see you hiding it under your coat. Give it—sir please! Just … hand it—*oof*—over! it's for your own … good! Orderly, please!

<ahem>

Moving on. Those of you doubled over and moaning from obvious intestinal distress: I'm very sorry your tummies hurt, but it really is your own fault. Next time show some restraint when all your tomatoes ripen at the same time … I don't know, make pasta sauce or something. Keep some in your car to throw at drivers who can't put their phones down

—

Aaand, sunburns! All of you who can correctly distinguish and apply a hundred different fertilizers, soil amendments and pesticides but still can't seem to figure out how to open a bottle of sunscreen. Please line up in order of severity from rosy to boiled lobster.

Oh, dear. Looks like we have some frostbites, too.

Okay, same deal: line up in order of severity, from numb white to … um, unboiled lobster. And I don't care if your pruning guide recommends winter pruning, next time at least look at the damn thermometer. Anything with a negative sign means stay the hell inside and eat soup.

And finally—at least I believe this should cover the rest of you: everyone who has sustained injuries to his/her pride or ego, say from an insufferable neighbor's lush lawn, seemingly immortal *Daphne odora*, or superior, blemish free rose, please leave the emergency room service to those with serious physical injuries, like this gentleman here.

Sir, you look to be suffering a great deal of head pain, what happened? … I see … wow, not even black spot, huh? … and fragrant, too? Well, I stand corrected, your head trauma may well be induced by your neighbor's inexcusably perfect tea roses. Right this way—step aside, people! Good lord, and she never even prunes them!? Now *my* head hurts …

Reason #15

<u>WHAT IS 7?</u>

Horticulture, like any other venture that does not find sufficiently buoyant validation from the rest of the world to keep its own ego afloat, has, over time, come to surround itself with a patchwork protective shell of jargon. This, the better to fluster whatever disrespectful outsider has the gall to question the merit of a life spent pulling weeds. It is simultaneously a childish plea for acknowledgment and a defensive barrier against our own feelings of self-doubt. The big words make us feel important. Without them, we'd be little more than overgrown kids running around outside picking flowers while the actual adults try to get some work done.

If you are to enter the minefield of gardening, you

will suffer this jargon to fly up into your face like a rake stepped-upon. It's everywhere. It chokes our language with pervasive contradictions, mispronunciations, best-guess spellings and faithfully-propagated misunderstandings. Most of which confounding principles are epitomized by that most vexing of terms: the semantic hot-potato that is "hardiness".

Not surprisingly, most new gardeners express some confusion over the word "hardy", which they inevitably encounter through reference books, plant tags, or in conversation with garden center employees. This initial misunderstanding stems from the fact that when we speak of "hardiness" in human terms, it is a qualitative trait, something possessed in varying degrees by individuals who are more or less likely, say, to survive a dogsled race through the Yukon. The victor of said race might be hailed as "one *hardy* sumbitch", while the participant who backed out upon discovering the dogsled to be neither heated nor chauffeured would not be described as especially hardy. In between is every poor frostbit bastard who crashed the sled, caught pneumonia or stopped off for an amputation or two along the way. These also-rans could rank anywhere from "pretty hardy" to "not all that hardy" or anywhere else along a broad, subjective spectrum of human hardiness. A spectrum which, ultimately, is not all that important, because "hardy" is just one of many, many adjectives we can choose from in characterizing our fellow humans.

But when our novice gardener hears "hardiness" bandied about down at the nursery, it somehow takes on more importance even as its definition recoils, hisses and ducks under a heavy rock, proving more elusive than your average trait. It seems important because a plant's mortal fate would appear to be dependent upon a correct deciphering of this jargon; and more elusive, because while everyone is technically speaking the same word, no one seems to be saying the same thing.

To many, this ambiguity is simply unacceptable. These are the people who willfully continue to use 'hardy' in the human sense, and can be heard requesting 'hardy' plants as though laying odds on the aforementioned dogsled racers; they want the toughest sumbitch they can find. Others have allowed that hardy might mean something different to plants, but they've gone and filled in the blanks all wrong. This type will leap erratically from one made-up definition to another, using hardy as a catch-all term for any desirable plant trait.

Only years of experience as a gardening translator have allowed me to decipher these many implied meanings of 'hardy', including, but not limited to: low-maintenance, structurally sound, tall, resilient, quick-to-establish, possessed of thick cuticle, able to withstand frequent assault by swinging metal gate, suitable for making cordage, able to withstand frequent assault by cat, fire-resistant, producing large fruit, evergreen, free-flowering, and once, confusingly, a customer who requested a particularly "hearty/hardy" variety of potato. Which or whatever she meant I'll never know. I have to draw the line somewhere. I'm sorry, we don't carry potatoes.

As determined gardeners catch on that "hardy" might be *somewhat* less random than all that, they often fall to the assumption that hardiness is a binary system, wherein any given plant is either 1.) Hardy, or 2.) Not hardy, with no funny business in between. This particular rose? Hardy. This *Brugmansia*? Not Hardy. In this arrangement, plants in category (1) will survive, and plants in category (2) will not. It's that simple. Why won't they survive? Because they're not hardy. Why aren't they hardy? Because they won't survive. A binary classification such as this is blessedly straightforward, and even more blessedly naïve. It falls to pieces under the slightest breath of inquiry, particularly with regards to location.

Let's say I'm told that my favorite ornamental banana is 1.) Hardy. Okay, fine, but suppose I purchase it here in Seattle and then take it home to my dogsled training compound in the Yukon, does this "hardy" attribute travel with it? Or does it now undergo some quantum weirdness where it is both hardy and not hardy, depending on location? Just because a plant's odds for survival are reasonable in the maritime Northwest, surely does not guarantee its success in the Canadian arctic. So now the jargon becomes muddied (muddy jargon=margon?). Hardy, but hardy *where*? And this is where zones come in.

Many prospective gardeners tap out at this point. I cannot blame them, or you, for doing so. In fact, just go ahead and stop reading now, you'll save yourself untold consternation, (and who couldn't do with a bit less of *that* -sternation).

Know your zone. What's your zone? Which *zone* are you *in*? Battle zone? End zone? Danger zone? Calzone? That nameless region of unmatched efficacy and productivity known as *The* Zone? One of the select few retail outlets or restaurants specialized enough to warrant 'zone'hood? *Are you stuffing your face down at the WaffleZone?*

Nothing so exciting, I'm afraid. We're talking USDA hardiness zones, to which most plants are ascribed membership. This system shatters the global duality of hardy/not hardy into various geographically and climatically defined regions of hardy/not hardy duality. These regions are numbered 1-13. Except that wasn't quite enough, so they split each zone into (a)s and (b)s. Much better. Now, suppose a plant is said to be hardy to zone 8b. Consulting my USDA map, I see that zone 8b corresponds to an average low temperature extreme of 15-20°F. What does this mean? It means next to nothing. Because sometimes a plant proclaimed hardy to zone 8b will power through a Winter blast of 8°F, and sometimes the same plant will give up the ghost when the mercury dips below 30. Why? Because they're plants, and if plants were people they'd be just like us: unpredictable, highly variable, and generally a pain in the ass.

To combat perceived shortcomings in the USDA system, various other hardiness zones have been proposed and rolled out with similarly lofty aims and to similarly maddening results. Not only do these systems fail to satisfy the angsty gardener's desire to know with certainty a plant's fate, each one moves the "hardy" concept further from our ideal binary truth and deeper into murky relativistic waters. Now we have to clarify, "Hardy" where? "Hardy" by which zone system? Furthermore, since other zone paradigms often employ the same numerals to categorize their zones, the unsettling semantic ambiguity now spills over from the linguistic to the mathematical, until we begin to question the very meaning and existence of numbers themselves, e.g.:

> *The tag says hardy to zone 7.*
> *But what does it mean by "7"? Which 7?*
> *What do you mean, "which 7"? 7 is 7.*
> *I don't know, is it? What is "7", really?*
> *WHAT IS 7!?*

And since any and all of these drunkenly parallel systems can simultaneously fail to predict a given plant's performance, it becomes far simpler and less stressful to embrace a zennish sort of paradox: all plants are hardy, and no plants are hardy. Just as we can never know for certain our own odds of survival beyond this moment, so too we must learn to accept fate when it comes for our so-called "hardy" banana.

Say it with a placid little smile: all plants are hardy and no plants are hardy. All plants live and all plants die.

All the same, I think I'll leave my banana behind when I return to the Yukon for this year's dogsledding season. It's about as hardy as I am.

Reason #16

<u>Self-Defense</u>

Look, if you really must go through with this gardening thing—highly discouraged, by the way—do me a favor, do yourself a favor, and at least learn some basic self-defense. That's right, you heard me. You think the horticultural world is all iced tea and billowy willows and scented blossoms on summer eves? It's not. I mean, there *is* iced tea … and there are a fair amount of scented blossoms, but—never mind, that's not the point. There's other stuff too, bad stuff—just come over here, would you?

All right, now before you learn how to protect yourself in the garden, you're going to want to loosen up a bit. Get limber. Stretch. That's right. Oh—well, jumping jacks aren't absolutely necessary, but—no, that's fine, if you want to … I'll just wait until you're done.

…

Someone's enthusiastic about jumping jacks—Okay, that's enough warming up!

Now, the first thing you have to realize is this: plants are not your friends. I hate to break that to you. They want nothing to do with you. They will, in fact, hurt you in order to make this preference known. They *want you to go away.* Unless you're a hummingbird, in which case—wait— you're not … are you? No? Well, I don't know, I thought maybe that's what all the jumping jacks were about. No? Okay. Well, seeing as you're *not* a hummingbird, or a bumble bee, or a moth, or any other pollinating whatnot, you have precious little co-evolutionary equity built up with plants. You belong, rather, to that class of big, lumbering, masticating animals, against which plants spent millions of years developing guerrilla tactics to keep themselves from being unduly ingested. Sorry, but it's true.

They have a whole *arsenal* of weapons you are just not prepared to deal with. Thorns, toxins, poisons, spikes, allergens, hallucinogenic compounds, bad smells, glass-like hypodermic syringes that break off when you touch them and inject stinging chemicals under your skin (yeah, that's how nettles get up in your business); indentured bacterial hordes, razor sharp leaf margins, phytophotodermatitis (which more or less turns you into a vampire); needles, irritating sap, land mines maybe, um, napalm ... probably, thorns—did I mention thorns already? Good, because THORNS, for real. Uh, let's see, ballistic pine cones. Submarines? Would anyone believe plants employ submarines in their defense? No? Yeah, probably not submarines. But for sure they use sleeper-cells of covert agents—what, did you think all those unassuming houseplants were somehow neutral in all this?

That's what they *want* you to think.

And there's your first mistake. Never assume a plant is innocent. No matter how soft and sweet and pretty. Some will hurt you, some will annoy you, and some will kill you. Some will betray you. Some set their tendrils upon empire, tearing across the yard like Alexander the Great as soon as root touches soil. Some will toy with your affections, stringing you along on promises of heaven scent or luscious fruit, but in the end requiting your love with nought but thirst and petulance and the occupation of valuable space. Some just sit there, biding their time. But never doubt they've all got some way to shank you as soon as you turn your back. Natural selection carved shivs for the plant kingdom and left instructions: don't trust anybody, least of all those big apes in the funny hats.

It stands to reason then, that your first, best tactic is evasion. Do not engage the opponent on their own terms. Do not bring a hori-hori knife to a gun fight. Make stealth your idiom; your presence must be no more than the whisper of a rumor of a ninja's shadow … at night. Got it?

Okay then, good, I think we're ready. Why don't you go ahead and step into the garden now—whoa, whoa, whoa! Not like that, you dunce! Slowly! Scout it out first. That was the worst ninja shadow I've ever seen. You see this, here? You darn near walked into a rose bush. These things are like the royal guard of the plant kingdom. They're everywhere, and once they grab hold, damned if they'll let go. I've got a buddy who's still stuck in a rose bush. Going on three years now. I visit him once a week to bring food and water. It's sad, but it's the life he chose. You too, if you're not careful.

There you go, that's better. Just have a look around. Now, they're already aware of you, so I wouldn't bother trying to be invisible anymore … um, that means you can stop trying to hide behind me. Yes, I see, that's very stealthy of you, but please stop. Sometimes they know you're coming before you do. I don't know how. The garden, even if it's on your own so-called property, belongs to the plants. It is *their* territory and you'd do well to concede that.

All right, now do a quick survey. Anything stand out? Take a look at that *Miscanthus* there. Just a grass, right? Gently rustling in the breeze. "Come on over," it's saying, "come sway with me," and then—*shiiing!* Slice you up like a samurai. Don't mess with grasses. Say it out loud … *don't mess with grasses*. Good. Now, how about over here? Euphorbias, Hellebores, *Daphne* … lovely plants, really, very pretty. Pretty POISONOUS—ha! HA! Why aren't you laughing? That was funny. But seriously— poisonous. Plants are like snakes: unless you know for certain, just assume bad things will happen if you get grabby.

Even stuff we grow for food can turn on you. Look over there: rhubarb. Do you like rhubarb? Mmm, strawberry rhubarb pie, right? Rhubarb and … um, I got nothing, I can't think of what else you would use rhubarb for. Maybe some sort of bracing, moonshine rhubarb brandy? Sun-dried rhubarb on pizza? I don't know. Whatever you do with it, just make sure you eat the part of rhubarb that's FOOD and not the part that's POISON! *Becauseit'sgotBOTH!* HA!

You look a little shaken-up, do you want to take a short break? Here, why don't you go ahead and pull a few weeds, that always helps me relax. There's a little patch of shotweed over here, that pulls out pretty easily … nice and calming—*except the part where it fires tiny seeds like missiles straight into your eye at the slightest touch!* HA! Heh-heh, okay you walked right into that one.

You're going to want to want to stop flailing around now; there's a *Yucca* right in front of you. You think shotweed makes your eyes water, wait until you impale your retina on a yucca blade. Skewer you like a kabob. Wanna see my yucca scars? Too bad, here they are … yep, and here … aaand over here … aaand these bad boys right here. And then on the other side—Okay, okay, I get it, you've had enough.

Well it doesn't matter, because *now we've got barberry incoming*! Let's see your combat roll: *go! NOW!*

No, no, no! *Away* from the barberry, not *into* it! Retreat! Retreat!

…

Are you hurt? C'mon, let's take a look. Ohhh, boy,

that is a wicked thorn. Didn't I mention thorns? No, I'd leave it in your forehead for now, it's just gonna bleed if you take it out. Consider it a reminder. A reminder to not suck so much.

So ... whenever you're done crying, we can continue. That's better. Now, you must always remember, a garden is more than just the plants you take home and shove in the ground. It is dynamic; it is an open system. A garden is an anything-goes arena where challengers may spring up at any time from within or without to try their hand at defeating the human overlord. *You* are their common enemy. An attack could come from a seemingly mild-mannered perennial you bought at the garden center (personally, I don't trust all these *Heucheras* ... they're up to something, I can tell) or from some malevolent, invasive—well, speak of the devil—*Shhh! Get down. Get down!*

Okay, this is what I was talking about—no, don't turn around! There's a Himalayan blackberry vine creeping up behind you. Don't panic, you fool! It can sense fear. Just listen to me. Now, obviously you didn't plant an invasive blackberry in your garden, but here it is all the same. These guys don't often wait for an invitation. So, what do you do? You can't let it continue, or your garden will be bramble by next week. This is one of those occasions where you're going to have to go on the offensive. Get back here, you coward! Here: choose your gloves and choose your weapon. Don't worry, the gloves are just a formality; there's no armor in the world that can stop a well-placed blackberry thorn. You're going to suffer casualties, get used to it.

Okay, you're going with the leather gloves and the machete? I admire your style. At the same time, I have a very real fear that you may not return with all four limbs—never mind, go, now! Attack! Now! Anytime! All right, now! Here we go!

...

I can't help but notice you're not attacking. Not having second thoughts about this, are you? Cold feet? Look at me, you pansy! That blackberry is barely two feet from the path. If you don't suck it up and take it out now, we'll all be dodging blackberry daggers by nightfall, understand? Okay, good. Now go! Attack!

Good, that's good; keep at it! Ooh! No, not like that— watch your back! Don't grab it, remeber what I said about the gloves, they're useless! You're in too deep! Pull out, pull out! Ooh, I can't watch ... What the—how did the blackberry get your machete!? No, don't struggle—stop moving! It'll just tighten its grip.

…

Well, that certainly could have gone better.

It looks like you're stuck. Are you stuck? Okay, that's what I thought.

<sigh>

Look, it may be time to admit you just weren't cut out for this. Don't feel bad, not everyone has what it takes to be a gardener. Just sit tight, try to get comfortable. I'll bring you some food and water sometime tomorrow.

Reason #17

You're Doing It Wrong

All of it. Everything, anything—the whole gardening *thing*. You name it and you're almost certainly doing it wrong. Novice, amateur, enthusiast, professional, expert: none of you could get it right if your lives depended on it. Go back to knitting. Go back to fencing. Go back to competitive Scottish highland games. Whatever, I don't care; go back to doing anything at which you are not so laughably awful.

To start with, you're using the wrong tools. Those tools are garbage, you need these tools. This brand. You need to spend more money when you buy tools, this is your *garden* after all. Unless, of course, you're spending *too much* money when you buy tools (which you probably are), then you should spend less—it's just a *garden* after all.

Then get to know your tools. Know your forks. Know your rakes. It is very important that you can accurately differentiate between a shovel and spade. Here is a diagram. It could not be less important that you accurately differentiate a shovel from a wombat, just reach for the tool you feel is right for the job. Your pruners couldn't cut through spam, sharpen them immediately. Whoa! Now they're too sharp, that's very wrong. Name your tools; christen them. Label your tools with bright tape. Label your tools with a laser engraver. Mark them with blood. Don't label your tools, you're being ridiculous. The storage system you employ to organize and access your tools is a joke. Here, buy all the latest belt/bucket/box/gun-safe/bandolier tool-storage gadgets. Evaluate them. And then throw them all away. Real gardeners hire a caddy to carry around their tools and offer appropriate tool suggestions. Real gardeners shoulder a quiver. *Pssh!* Real gardeners don't use tools.

Your gardening philosophy is juvenile. You have no ideas of your own and it is wrong to imitate. You must find your own way; be an innovator. Unless you have no ideas of your own, then there's nothing wrong with imitating the more creative, better minds in the field (which is all of them).

Imitation is the sincerest form of flattery. Innovation is the sincerest form of bullshit.

And those plants in your garden? All wrong. What were you thinking? No one plants roses anymore. No one. These perennials here are trendy, those are old-fashioned, and these are invasive. Ha! And those are just ugly. Why aren't there any roses? You can't have a garden without roses.

No, *I* never use fertilizer. I use composted edamame husks exclusively.

Surely you see that your plant selections are environmentally unsound, aesthetically offensive, and prone to disease. They are tacky. They are not adequately drought tolerant. They are genetically modified and *not grown organically?* You ass, you are worse than Satan. Your plants are all dying, and it's your fault. You deserve it. Well, no wonder your plants are dying, they have not been sufficiently genetically modified! And where's the fertilizer?

Your taste in plants is … ugh—just wrong. You need more structure, more evergreen plants, more bulbs—oh, these bulbs are all planted at the wrong depth, by the way. And they're the wrong bulbs. And it's the wrong time of year to be planting bulbs in the first place. Where was I? Oh yes, you need more texture, more color, more edibles, more deciduous plants, and maybe more rusted scrap metal to provide a stolid counterpoint to the verdant plant material. But sometimes less is more. That's too many edibles, all the fruit will just go to waste. It will attract disease and pests. It will rot and attract rats and rabid hyenas and Hitchcock's Birds. Tear them all out. Fill in with annuals. No, I mean *annuals,* like good annuals, not—ow! I just cut myself on some damn piece of rusted metal! Your garden is a junk yard. And why are you using annuals? No one plants annuals.

Oh, and everything about your technique is wrong. To begin with, you have no skill with pruners and no eye for form. You are not so much pruning as engaging in serial murder. All of your cuts will result in diseased wood. None of them will heal properly. They will sucker aggressively with weak wood, which will split and fall onto your house in the slightest breeze. Your children are at risk. You are not pruning, you are incurring liability. The act, as you perform it, is ethically and morally unjustifiable.

Clean your pruners with rubbing alcohol. Clean them with bleach. Clean them with peppermint schnapps, but never, ever, ever use bleach. You know what, don't bother cleaning your pruners, it's a waste of time.

You are cutting at the wrong angle. Like this, see? No, not like that. Forget it. Just hack the bastards back once a year to keep 'em in check.

Those weeds will just come right back if you keep weeding like that. Or like that. You have the wrong weeding tool. All weeding tools are gimmicks. What you need is a hori-hori knife. What you need is a screwdriver. What you need is a melon-baller. Just spray them. Just use your goddamn hands. Ack! That spray will kill you. It will kill me! That one will sterilize you. Yes, and that one will turn baby owls highlighter yellow. You're a monster. Just leave the weeds where they are, they have just as much a right to be here as any other plant. I mean, what exactly is a weed, anyway? THAT! THAT is a weed. Kill it. Get rid of it now. But not *right* now—if you pull weeds now, they'll just spread even more. Do it later. But don't wait too long. Shoot, now there are weeds everywhere. Your garden looks like an abandoned lot.

Your plants are flopping everywhere; tie them up. Be sure to use the right material. All of the following materials are wrong for tying up plants, but some of them are not wrong: string, any kind of twine, yarn, wire, hemp, tendon, ribbon, old t-shirts, nylons, braided yucca fiber, bungie cords, socks, jute, flexible plastic, friendship bracelets, and rubber bands. You should never tie up a plant. It is wrong to do so. But then, of course, you *should* tie up some plants, and when you do use good twine or an old t-shirt.

Speaking of t-shirts, how many times do I have to tell you, you're wearing the wrong clothes for gardening. Are you *trying* to get a sunburn? Put on more clothes. Wear a shawl, carry a parasol. Always use leather. Unless you object to murder, in which case use cotton. But cotton is unsustainable, so use, I don't know, lycra. Jeez, you look fat in lycra. Wear a hat. No, not *that* hat, you look ridiculous. But who cares what you look like? Who cares what others think? Is this the only vest you have? Other people can *see* you, you know. You're going to need more and better vests. These are to be your proudest uniform. Don't be ashamed, just go shirtless. Just go naked. It is wrong to put clothes between your skin and the soil. I swear to god, if I see another gardener wearing a vest I'm going to—those gloves will give you a rash, by the way. And those will offend the delicate sensibilities of your tea roses. Try sheepskin. Try latex. The only gloves to wear are

Atlas gloves. The only gloves to wear are catchers' mitts. Everything else is wrong. Those boots will give you blisters. Just go barefoot. Always wear close-toed shoes. I swear by cowboy boots. I swear by clogs. I swear by scuba flippers. No, that's the wrong brand of clogs. Only idiots wear clogs.

What did you just say? That's what I thought—you're saying it wrong. It's pronounced *"Agastache"* not "Agastache", and it's **_HEMEROCALLIS_** not "Hemerocallis". My god, you sound like a dolt. Stick with common names. Make up your own common names. Only amateurs use common names. I have no idea what you're talking about. Would it kill you to learn some Latin? Slow down there, poindexter, now you sound like a snob. I have no idea what you're talking about.

I'm sorry, I just have *no* idea what you're talking about.

Even your attitude is wrong. Gardening is all about a state of mind. Breathe deeply and be one with the plants, be one with the soil. It is wrong to harm any living thing. Unless the living thing is harmful, then, for god's sake, why aren't you harming it faster? Kill the weeds, kill the bugs, kill the deer, kill the neighborhood kids when they trample through your beds. Protect your little patch of dirt because it's all you have in this world.

Your garden is a gift to the world.

Breathe. Breathe—no, not like that. Breathe *correctly*. In … out … in—oh forget it, you're a waste of breath.

Try yoga. If you're not doing yoga, you're certainly doing it wrong.

Quit tying yourself in a knot, what you need to do is read more. You need to follow gardening blogs and go to book-signings and acquire reference books and then bookmark them for easy reference. No, not that book, that book is a joke, don't use that one. Anyone who writes a book is a charlatan. Anyone who reads it is a sucker. Try to forget everything you just read.

Now start over. Read weekly columns and almanacs and magazines and "get ideas". Buy books promising fresh design ideas. Buy books promising fresh takes on the perennial border. Buy any book with the word "fresh" in the title. Here are the top twenty recommended gardening books. Some are funny, some are wise, some are insightful. All are cherished; all are worthless. Here are the twenty worst. Buy those too. Here are 300 gardening books so devoid of character as to dodge judgment altogether. Buy them anyway. Buy them all.

And then bury them in the garden, which is where you should have been all along. Bury this book, then buy it again. The author is full of quackgrass. Stop reading and start gardening.

Not like that, you're doing it wrong.

Reason #18
<u>Paparazzi</u>

Hurry! Jump in, quick! Just ignore the cameras! *No, I'm sorry folks, we've got nothing for you tonight—just a night on the town. No comment. No comment. No, sorry. No comment!* Come on, you, shut the door! *<Sigh>* Every single time. Driver! Get us out of here. I don't care … anywhere.

Look, it's like this—sorry, you want some scotch, perrier, something? Energy drink? Fresh fig-arita? Figs are from my garden … no? All right, suit yourself.

Okay—so I guess the real question you need to ask yourself, when considering gardening as a profession or hobby is: can you handle … *this*? The fame, the glitz, the three-ring circus of fans, cameras and adoration; the drugs (god, I take so much ibuprofen, you wouldn't believe) the orgie—I mean garden tours. It never ends, it never—sorry, I'm gonna have some brandy, you sure you don't want any? Cognac? Ouzo? Tequila? I've got limes here, somewhere …

Anyway, I think the world just cares so much about gardeners. And that's fair; it's only the *most* important job, right? I mean, why do you think every good TV drama worth watching is centered around gardening? … Huh? I don't know, there's like, a lot of them—stop interrupting. So TV, magazines, social media, those paparazzi scum—they're all working together to put your face, your lifestyle out there. You pulling weeds … uh, you pushing your wheelbarrow— whatever—to put *you* squarely in the public eye. You become this, like, persona that may or may not resemble who you really are. But, so everyone sees that awesome, fake, persona and everyone wants a piece of it. They want to be you, or at least near you. They think *you're* the lucky one.

Picture it: they're driving by on their way to the office some morning. Got their suit and tie, briefcase, drive-thru coffee, uh, uh, shoeshine, rolodex—I don't know what the hell they bring to the office—and there *you* are out in the sunshine, tying up *Clematis* or something, wearing some crazy get up like the rock-star they wanted to be when they were a kid. Is that *Jimi Hendrix* pruning roses? Y'know? What's *Prince* doing in the herb garden? Goddamn. Crazy hats. And, like, is that a whole *pitcher* of iced tea on the table? That kind of excess, that pig-in-shit revelry they want so bad. They want to roll in it. You've got the life they want to live.

Think about it, if any of those poor bastards out there want, like, say a beet, they gotta put on pants, drive to the grocery store and buy some godawful beet from the shelf. Checker up front doesn't even know what a beet is—but anytime you want a beet, you don't need pants! You freakin' *never need pants*. Who *are* you? Y'know? What *world* do you live in? Cuz it's not the same one they do. They can't *fathom* that kind of—you just bend over and pull it out of the ground —speaking of which … you want a beet? Just picked em this morning. No? Goes great with, like … oh, what else do I have in here … Midori? What the hell is that? Driver! Did you put Midori in the limo mini-fridge? What's this green stuff? Melon!? Really? No, no, I'll give it a shot.

…

Ugh, sorry—did you want some? Not so great with

the beets, but see, no one's going to tell me what to do. Just like no one's going to tell you what to do. And that's why you've got to decide. Can you handle this? Can you make the right choices? Think of all the gardeners before you who just couldn't deal with the lifestyle. Better gardeners than you— no offense—who couldn't take the pressure. Legends. Cameras and microphones leering over their shoulder, 24/7. "Why are you planting bush beans and not pole beans?" Y'know? Or, like, "How do you get dandelions out?" "What brand of gloves are those?" God, that's another thing. The endorsements. Whore. You're a whore. Get used to it. Look at this … yeah, see those? Knee pads. I have to wear them every time I'm in public. It's in my contract. My own line of knee pads. I wear 'em to the movies. To dinner. They don't even work; I hate these things. Here, roll down the window.

Hey ladies! Want some knee pads? Take 'em! We'll be at the flower show, later, if you're looking for fun.

God, jeez. Yeah, there's dignity for you. You see that? Now they'll probably follow the limo until I sign the damn things.

<Sigh>

Is it worth it? Well, what's the alternative? What else

are you going to be? An athlete? An astronaut? A movie star? A teacher? You gonna be able to look yourself in the mirror every morning knowing that you're out there *teaching* people? Flying off to the moon? Yeah, that's noble. I mean, everyone's gotta decide for themselves, but someone's gotta step up and live life in the spotlight and it may as well be you and me. We *change* the world, what we do. We grow the onions, if you get my drift. We plant the petunias, if you will. Right? Right? And if the price we pay is having to stare at paparazzi shots of our tool sheds on the cover of checkout line tabloids, then so be it. It's what we do. It's what we do. It's! What! We! Do! We mow the lawn! We prune the pear trees! We make *pickles* out of *cucumbers*! We can say *Hamamelis*! We know—we *know* what a rutabaga is! And *we* divide the @#$%!%^# IRISES! IRISES!! *IRISES*!!! MNNNNNN—@^%$@ #$#@ DAY-LILIES!!! AAHH!

...

Sorry, what were we talking about?

I don't know, sometimes I love it—hey, if I pop a bottle of champagne, will you have some? C'mon, now, you can't say no, this bottle was a gift from the King of ... Chile. Wait, does Chile have a king? Probably not, huh? Well, who the hell gave me the champagne? Said he was the King of something ... Oh well.

I mean, it was fun at first. Going to the hort. society plant sales and being mobbed. Signing people's hats. The screaming fans at the mall when someone sees your Felcos. Makes you feel loved, I guess. Important, anyway, like a— Okay—this is clearly not champagne. It's ... I don't know, what does that taste like? Absinthe!? Whoa, where the *hell* was that King from? Whoops. Well, this'll be an interesting flower show, anyway.

So but sometimes, y'know, I just want to sleep. I want to wake up in my own bed. I want to rake the leaves in peace without narrated tour buses driving by asking me to wave. I want to get back to the *gardening,* y'know? That gets lost along the way. What it means to plant a tree; to water it; to watch it grow. To lay down mulch like a blanket, tucking in your perfect, sweet little *garden*—<sob>—sorry, give me a minute ... To clip the hedge without groupies begging for the clippings. It's just boxwood for crying out loud! To have birds splashing in your birdbath instead of creepy stalkers who can't comprehend a restraining order. Yeah, it happens. Oh, man, this one poor guy was actually *licking* the syrup from my hummingbird feeder. Ugh. It's a weird business. A weird life. And it takes its toll, y'kow? All the digging, lifting, crawling on hands-and-knees. All the late nights and bottles of absinthe … wow, was that the whole bottle? Well, you had some, too, right?

Just fuel for the fire. You're a rock-star now.

Okay, looks like we're at the flower show, you ready? Sunglasses? Hat? Vest? Pants? Damn straight, *you* don't need pants. Not when you work with plants. All right, champ, get out there and smile.

Reason #19

<u>Harbingers</u>

If only one warning should find your ears, dear reader, let it be the following. If all my cautionary prattle slips through the sieve of your consciousness but for one lump of wisdom, let that lump be this. If you simply cannot take any more of this incessant finger wagging, then fine! but heed one last earnest plea. If you want me to get to the point already, here it is:

Oh, for the love of all that is good and right in the world, spare yourself the agony of mums!

Those puffballs of formless, default color; those harbingers of senile Autumn and Winter; those late season bench-warmers who have no real business in the gardening milieu but to remind us that, long before our gardens coughed and wheezed through Summer drought, powdered with mildew and desperate for any transfusion of color; long before we pulled carrots from Grandma's vegetable bed as children; long before our species named the seasons and gave them suitable crops—the hands of the clock were already wound and spinning down. And it is none but the mums who toll the moaning bell at the top of the hour, every hour—a gonging portent of the unceasing cycle of nature to which we are subject but cannot, as individuals, ever belong.

Prior to this unwanted visitation of flowery pestilence upon garden centers the world over, a given year's parade of leaf and bloom—in new permutations, at slightly different times, always with new varieties in a fresh new context—may propagate the illusion that this year, things will be different. This year, we may finally escape the confines of seasonality and mortality to flourish evermore in the breathtaking, rapturous garden of our minds eye. At long last, we will achieve horticultural enlightenment. With a golden explosion, this floral divinity will propagate through the metaphysical to suffuse our corporeal existence. This year, dare I say, we will become as gods …

But then the chrysanthemums show up.

And no, this year will not be any different; what fools we were. The sun will dip lower, the shadows yawn wider and, sooner or later, the killing frost will find you and yours. All is temporary. All is fleeting and lonely and doomed.

God damn thee, mums! How can we willfully suspend our disbelief in time's arrow with your brittle stems snapping off and littering the ground like corpses? How can we pretend our own Winters will never come? How can we plan for any sort of future with your brash hues slapping us in the face like a tether-ball every September? Your clumsy swaths of color are vomited forth like the never-ending kerchief from a funnyman's mouth. You are an unwelcome act, a tired bit. You are a clowny dirge.

I ask of you, reader, what other endeavor's hope and joy is so reliably and repeatedly snuffed out by such a tide of rainbow melancholy as washes in, each year, with the mums? What similarly cursed pursuit's death knell sounds with such jarring, kindergarten joviality? What other works of grace and beauty and fruitful toil are thus ushered out the door by such bumbling, slapstick dunces as mums?

None.

Mums are naught but a bad punchline interjected into

an otherwise elegant, moving narration. They are a whoopy-cushion slipped onto the seat as the gardener collapses into tired reflection at season's end. They are a tacky, token retirement gift doled out by a faceless employer at the conclusion of a long career, which serves only to trivialize the great and diligent work of a lifetime. They are the bright and cherubic imps of death, together dragging Winter's scythe behind and giggling at the tenuous frailty of it all.

And now, unless you stop and avert your stride from the quicksand which sprawls unseen all across the path of gardening, those evil clown mums are coming ... for *you*.

Reason #20

<u>I Can Quit Any Time</u>

—Said the hunchbacked, arthritic, sun-leathered, delusional thirty-something who accidentally made a career out of gardening.

But the truth is, I can't just quit this inglorious, aching, annoyingly satisfying life any more than I could quit myself. All the seeds I have planted, the gardens I have tended, the plants I have sold, are now a part of me. When one of these languishes—when one dies, when one flourishes, or blossoms, or brings joy—it, in some small but meaningful way, connects me to a larger world, across time and space and kingdoms of life. Plants and their remarkable diversity, their unknowable but wonderful separateness from man, their potential for beauty and frustration, are the medium through which I and all gardeners shout, ceaselessly and to anyone who will listen, every unspeakable angst and urge and joy of existence.

Even on mornings when I can barely get out of bed— if the dawn's glow happens to slant just so through the blinds, it rouses me with the reminder that there is still sunlight to catch. Never mind that the flesh is weak, for if the sun and soil are willing, there is clearly and always more gardening to be done.

The motive force of this compulsion is difficult to articulate, but can perhaps best be approximated as a sort of fetishised existential guilt. Floundering for meaning in this current, ensiliconed age, I once chanced upon a long, strong green vine, which disappeared above me and below. I clung tightly to it, and its own tendrils wound about my hands. Now, I cannot bring myself to sever whatever this real or imagined horticultural tendon is, which reaches back into our species deep history to provide anchorage and flexion to our modern might. If I let go and walked away, it would be to the abandonment of the only heritage I have ever strongly felt. And thus the guilt. What sort of person would I be if the sun rose above the trees to find my hand empty and clean, the ground fallow and tending to feral? It is not too much of a stretch to suggest that I might feel more animal than human, more criminal than free. So I get out of bed, ice my back, take an ibuprofen, and plant some collard greens. I prune a client's rose. I explain once more and patiently the difference between pansy and viola. I wait for rain.

As to the ultimate origin of my own fixation, I cannot say for certain, though I suspect it may lie, overgrown, in an abandoned orchard near the banks of a muddy slough where I spent my youth. There, whatever fruit still grows, falls heavy to the fertile ground below, to be eaten, or decomposed, or germinated anew by whatever posterity possesses humor and tenacity enough to look past however many reasons not to garden for the one, much better reason to do so.

May you find your own.

THE END

About the Author

Luke Ruggenberg lives in the Pacific Northwest. He studied Botany at a middling University and then crash-landed in the horticulture industry, where he has since worked as a gardener and nurseryman for nearly a decade. He currently tries to keep the plants alive at a small-but-mighty, independent Seattle garden center.

At home, Luke struggles to keep his own plants alive while trying valiantly to appreciate how lucky he is to have such a wonderful wife and daughter. He maintains a cheeky gardening blog to this effect entitled Fencebroke Promontory Gardens (fencebroke.blogspot.com).

Made in the USA
Monee, IL
14 July 2020